FROM DUNBAR TO DESTINY

FROM DUNBAR TO DESTINY

One Woman's Journey through Desegregation and Beyond

Shirley Robinson Sprinkles

From Dunbar to Destiny: One Woman's Journey through Desegregation and Beyond

License to reprint TIME/LIFE photo on cover granted by Getty Images

This book is dedicated to the memory of Morgan Maxwell, my first principal, who courageously fought for educational parity for Dunbar School's black students, and who admonished us all to "be the best!"

Contents

Part I
My Birth and Early Home Life

Part II
School and Community Life

Part III
Life in LA: My City by the Sea

Part IV
Marriage and Family

Part V
Making Texas My Home...Again

Part VI
My Children

Part VII
My Life Today

Preface

By the time the Warren Court began rearguing the landmark school desegregation case, *Brown v. Board of Education*, which was before it in the Supreme Court (1953), Tucson, Arizona's board of education, and its district superintendent, Robert Morrow, had already made up their minds: racially segregated education in Tucson's public schools would come to an abrupt halt—schools would be integrated. The first year of implementation of school desegregation there was 1951. I had spent the better part of seven years attending what was to me and about seven hundred other students the most beloved school in all the world, Paul Laurence Dunbar Elementary and Junior High. Paul Laurence was the black school located in the barrio on the west side of town. I was not happy with the board's decision. In fact, I can't remember anyone who, at the time, was gleeful about the forthcoming integration.

It was a time of mixed emotions—emotions that varied between schoolchildren and adults, alumni, taxpayers, and politicians. The forecast of greater and equal educational opportunity sounded so positive on the one hand; on the other was this thick, dark veil of uncertainty that accompanied such a monumental change. Initially, what we—the Dunbar community of students, teachers, and parents—felt was more akin to depression and deep sadness than to any other emotion. We were losing something that we cherished. The Fourteenth Amendment notwithstanding, we minority students did not feel "deprived of equal educational opportunities, even though the physical facilities and other 'tangible' factors may be equal."

It was the *in*tangibles that had us bummed out. Yes, it was those aspects of schooling that couldn't be measured by data: pride, love, community support and encouragement, friendships, school spirit, "family," and the most precious of all intangibles: dignity. The loss of these vital and sustaining life forces was the source of my (and others') deep anxiety and personal conflict. We had excellent teachers. New construction had improved our facilities and made life more comfortable on our campus. Our athletic teams were high-perform-ing winners in virtually all local and state competitions in which we were permitted to participate. The fine arts program was not lagging behind either. We enjoyed plays, choir, and band activities. Aside from hand-me-down, outdated textbooks, we did not feel in any way "deprived."

That was then. Looking back, I can now candidly state that what happened was the best thing that could have ever happened to me. My educational (and many other) opportunities did, indeed, expand—beyond my wildest dreams. Life for me took on new, exciting attri-butes after Dunbar, and as the lessons I've learned keep unfolding, life continues to amaze me. I'm so proud to have been a Dunbar student—so very, very proud. It was in that place that a solid founda-tion was laid in my soul for all that has followed.

There are many "Dunbar schools" in this country. Perhaps you, the reader of this book, may have attended one of them at one time in your own city. If so, I am confident that you will identify with many of the anecdotes that are highlighted in *From Dunbar to Destiny*. They are stories that characterized the culture of the "Dunbars," "Carvers," "Washingtons," "Wheatleys," and "Bethunes"—schools named for former slaves—that so many African Americans attended because they were the only schools that were available for blacks for so long. I believe that it is precisely because of our composite experiences in those settings of old that we who are black in this country have come through many generations of struggle for equality. Our successes were drawn by an indomitable spirit that was learned in those segregated schools: the spirit to work, help each other to survive, thrive, and excel in spite of difficult social and economic conditions.

On my own, without the solid educational and spiritual founda-tion I acquired in my youth, I know that I would never have achieved some of the amazing things that I have achieved in my lifetime. There's been a lot of help. I have not built castles, scaled lofty mountain peaks, or raised trillions to feed the poor. Nor have I earned a Nobel Prize for some monumentally worthy literary attainment. However, by most social and economic measures, what I've accomplished in my lifetime, considering the point from which I began, has been anything but average.

Along the way, I have done the ordinary things, too: I have raised four children to adulthood (and sometimes beyond); I have successfully mastered enough academia to earn four degrees from four different colleges and universities; I have worked happily in five careers, building one on top of the other; and I have purchased and lived in four lovely homes and bought six automobiles, some with partners, some alone.

Isn't it funny how a whole lifetime fits so snugly into one short paragraph?

Like most things in life, what you see on the surface is not the whole story. As Gustave Flaubert put it, "*Le bon dieu est dans le détail*" or, translated to English, "God is in the details."[1] Others, such as Michelangelo and the art historian Aby Warburg, are frequently quoted as having used a variant of this phrase: "The devil is in the details." "The devil is in the details" is a variant of the proverb, referring to a catch hidden in the details.

In reference to my life, I subscribe to both versions. As I share some of the details of my journey from Dunbar to my destiny, I will take you with me into the important caverns, deep valleys, and ditches and up some of the mountaintops that comprised my journey. Along the way, I invite you, the reader, to decide where and when these powerful forces (God and devil) were at work in my life.

Among those who choose to read my story, in part or in its entirety, I hope many will be teachers, parents, and students. Reading it will evoke nostalgic memories for those who have shared my experiences—old memories that will bring smiles (or grimaces) to your faces. For others, the stories will sound like current events, for there are still many unresolved social, relational, and cultural circumstances like the ones I faced that exist to this very day.

In any case, it is my fervent hope that by the time you reach the end, you will feel that the time spent reading will have been worthwhile. I also hope the read will be enjoyable.

1   Gregory Y. Titleman, *Random House Dictionary of Popular Proverbs and Sayings* (New York: Random House, 1996).

Acknowledgments

Special thanks to everyone who took time to read excerpts of my book. Your kind words of praise and encouragement, as well as the sessions of constructive criticism that you provided enabled me to keep moving forward. All of the staff at Wheatmark, Inc., especially Susan Wenger and Grael Norton, are in this group, along with copyeditors who contributed professional skill and editorial guidance throughout the process. From them I learned so much. My appreciation is boundless.

To my husband, Leo, I owe a special hug and thanks. You always had faith in me, believing always that the story was worthwhile, and lending a patient ear to the many readings and agonizing edits that I, a novice writer, subjected you to.

Thank you so much, Ernest Charles McCray. I kept a whole folder just full of your many witty and wise responses to my story's revelations, chapter by chapter, paragraph by paragraph. Because you are, yourself, such a talented writer, I valued your every word.

Rosetta Williams, you read the first sixty pages and thought I should publish the story. The seed was planted in that conversation. I never wanted to disappoint *you*!

Ralston Pitts, I have always admired your ability to think deeply and respond so intelligently and cogently to issues I've presented in our many dialogues about just about everything. Your wise analysis and special encouragement have helped me expand the boundaries of my memories. Seeing things through your perspectives has been most enlightening!

June O'Kelley Armstrong, my dear and constant friend, thanks for writing your thoughts and responses in the margins of the first draft manuscript, then for returning your copy to me when I had let my last copy slip out of my hands! Without you, important edits would not have been made.

Billie Cahill, thanks, my loyal, patient, and prudent friend. Your wise counsel in regards to sensitive parts of my recall remain as echoes in my consciousness. Only you could articulate what worried me most about the book. Just hearing it straight helped so much. Thank you!

Pat Davenport, my judicious and humorous counsel and friend. It was fun just laughing and exploring issues exposed in my story with you. You and James Hammond shared similar concerns and insights. You both helped so much!

Vonceil Weaver, your infectious enthusiasm has made me feel like a winner. Your smiling voice on the phone told me how entertaining the story was, and how much you enjoyed reliving so much of it across the pages. You have helped authenticate my memory of so much that happened so long ago. Thank you, friend.

Introduction

I was born February 6, 1938, into a deeply impoverished black family in the rural south: Greenville, Texas, to be exact. My mother was a teenager who finished high school at fifteen years old. She was brilliant, but she had no place to go. Her family could not afford to send her to college, though she dreamed of going to either Paul Quinn or Texas Christian College. My father, who was twenty-one when he married my fifteen-year-old, pregnant mother, had barely completed a third grade education. With virtually no skills beyond picking cotton, this couple set out to make a life for themselves and their new baby. Their destinies looked bleak from that starting point; but time, perseverance, and divine intervention altered their course, and a different story unfolded for them and for me, their second child.

That I am alive today, a well-educated, healthy, and relatively financially secure woman is no accident, nor is it a miracle. It is because good people took my hand to give me a lift up or got my attention at key times and gave me good advice and/or personal care. Inevitably, I will leave out someone's name who deserves to be included. I apologize up front for any unintentional lapses or gaps in my memory. A sixty-nine-year lifespan is really not so long anymore, but it is a long time to try to remember everything! In a world where many try hard not to get involved in the lives of others for a myriad of reasons—"too busy," "too tired," "not interested," "too broke," to name a few—I was lucky, from an early age, to have people who took the time and allowed themselves to be *interrupted* in order to help and positively influence me. In essence, I was hoisted onto the shoulders of many people so I could see where I might go if I stayed focused and kept my mistakes to a minimum. Without them, I shudder to think where I might have ended up.

I've often wondered why people bother to write autobiographies.

It seems such a self-serving activity. Most only tell the things that make the writer look good: chronicles of heroic deeds, gut-wrenching tales of outrunning poverty or brutality perpetrated by others. Hopefully, I will not fall into that style; I truly don't like it. Instead, I would like to introduce my readers to a host of my "angels"—real, live, people, blacks, whites, Latinos, Jews, Catholics, and Christians, who carried me across mental, psychological, physical, and even financial bridges and potential landmines while I searched for the right paths. They were, and still are, my heroes and heroines to whom I owe so much. They are family, friends, teachers, and perfect strangers. It was exposure to the people I will talk about in this story that contributed immeasurably to the encouragement I embraced, often through difficult, confusing times, to take the steps necessary to continue my journey forward. Their influence, regardless of the scope or magnitude of their deed, still imprints and resonates in my life. It is with humility and gratitude that I turn the spotlight on my angels and their contributions. They intervened and shaped the attitudes, habits, and moral values that were stepping-stones to the person that I have become.

Where I have deemed it prudent to do so, I have changed the names of some of the characters. Although the stories are true, I prefer to use discretion to protect anonymity in some cases. I seek no particular chronology; nor have I placed events and their angels in terms of significance. When one sews a beautiful quilt, he or she picks out the pieces that are essential to the design and tries to weave them in. How the pieces fit together in my story will be revealed largely by the reader's interpretation.

Part I

My Birth and Early Home Life

*You are the bows from which your children
as living arrows are sent forth.*

—Khalil Gibran

My Family

I was born just before my mother's eighteenth birthday. It was a cold, wet February night (the sixth of the month) in 1938 when Mama first felt pains that awakened her. Believing it to be just gas, Mama tried to ignore the discomfort and get back to sleep. But the pain was relentless. Eventually, she decided to get out of bed and sit for a spell on the "pot"—an indoor night jar that was situated in a corner near the bed for night use. The bathroom was an outdoor outhouse.

To her surprise, one push on her bowel delivered a baby girl...me. I wasn't due until the end of March. Surprise, surprise! It was a Sunday morning, and Daddy was not at home, as usual. Mama aroused my two-year-old brother, Carl Jr., and somehow made him understand to go next door and get Sister Emma, the local midwife. Somehow, help arrived. I was very tiny—only four and a half pounds. But I was healthy, although pretty ugly according to Mama.

There had been no preparation for my birth. Mama had planned to go to town the next week to buy blankets and diapers, but there was nothing on hand for a new baby. I was wrapped in a quilt until my grandmother could be summoned. This was my real, biological, grandmother, who had reconnected with Mama after a long absence from her life. She arrived with clean flour sacks and proceeded to sew my first "layette" of rough cotton gowns by hand. She sewed all day. When she left, I had four gowns and a handful of "diapers" in which to start life.

-My Mother-

Copply Williams was born in Neylandville, Texas. She was the second of three children born to Roger and Earlee Williams. Her sister, Rosetta, was just shy of two years older. A brother was born

when Copply was two, but he died when he was accidentally smothered while nursing his mother's breast in the parental bed. She had
fallen asleep, and the newborn child rolled under her tired body
and died there. Sadness and depression overcame and consumed my
maternal grandmother. She just couldn't get over the guilt she felt
for her son's death. For that, and who knows what other reasons, she
packed her few belongings in a knapsack one morning after Papa had
left for work in the fields, and took off walking across a field in the
opposite direction. It was the last time Copply would see her mother
for nearly ten years. The sight of watching her mother go, after telling
her little girls, "Stay here till your daddy gets back," was a memory
my mother never forgot.

All of her life, she wondered why she had been abandoned.
Although a reconciliation of sorts took place after several years of
absence, the relationship between my mother and her birth mother
was never genuinely close.

Meanwhile, Papa found a suitable widow in a nearby town, and
soon married her. She and her five children moved into the farm-
house with Copply, Rosetta, and Papa, and a new life began for all.
Big Mama, as I called her growing up, was Daisy Fields; she was a
short, thick woman with a sultry but warm demeanor, and she could
cook! Copply called her Mother, and as far as I ever heard, she never
called her anything else.

Copply was the youngest of all the children. The older girls did
all the housework, often "shooing" her out of their way. She was left
to do the only chore she remembers, churning butter on the front
porch. She admitted to eating as much as she churned. There was
plenty of sibling rivalry to go around. Papa was stern and took no
nonsense from any of the children, so Copply got her share of whuppin's right alongside the others, whether she was guilty or not. On the
other hand, Papa also protected her fiercely. No one was going to take
advantage of her.

Roger was a hardworking sharecropper. Everyone had to work to
keep food on the table. When Copply was big enough to go to the
field to pick cotton or to use a hoe for chopping, she was expected to
contribute her share. She learned quickly and soon stood out as an
asset when it came to labor. She was the *son*, metaphorically speaking,

that Papa never had. He took great pride in her prowess in the work-place! He boasted that she could out-pick any man in the field. She loved receiving his praise and would not disappoint him. She was a cotton-picking machine.

In the evenings, the kids would entertain each other playing dominoes and bid whist. Copply was a champ at both. When Uncle Tommy, her favorite of Papa's two brothers, was around, "Cope," as he called her, would sneak sips from his near-empty beer bottles. She acquired the taste for this beverage at an early age, though she suppressed her desire for it until much later in her life.

Copply was also very smart in school. She had special aptitude in mathematics and was often called up to higher grades in the small seg-regated schoolhouse that she attended, to "set down" older students in oral quizzes or chalkboard competitions. Her teachers loved to see her outdo really smart kids two and three grades ahead of her. She was passed two grades a year for three years. By age fourteen, she had passed every class offered in the small, local school and was eligible to graduate. After graduation, she had no place to go. Too poor to go away to college, she stayed around home. Soon she started going out with Carl Henry Robinson, my father. They married shortly after she met him.

Before my father, who was seven years her senior, Copply had never really dated anyone else. She'd never had a serious boyfriend. The only boy she ever talked to was John Faulk, an overweight, curly-haired boy who lived with his grandparents on the neighboring farm. They were in the same class in school. He liked her a lot and tried hard to get her attention, but she ignored his efforts. The more experienced one, Carl Henry, won her heart.

When Copply was fifteen years old, Carl Jr. was born. Copply was about as ill-prepared for marriage as one could be. She knew nothing about homemaking and even less about being a woman. Mama was not aware of how pretty she was. She had not been allowed to spend time looking in mirrors. She was clueless about feminine wiles and other attributes of womanly behavior. To say she was green would be an understatement. She used to laugh when she told us about those first few months of marriage; she was still wetting the bed at night! She was scared and confused. And soon she would be a mother.

She credited my paternal grandmother, Catherine Robinson, with saving her by guiding her through that malaise. Grandma Catherine was patient and kind. She had two daughters of her own near Mama's age: Minnie Lee and Ethyl. They were having children too. Grandma Catherine had her hands full!

Mama's life, which began in the state of Texas eighty-two years before her death, took many twists, turns, and tumbles before ending. She was a warrior, tough and resilient to the last breath. She was also an inspiration to dozens of people along the way, not the least of whom was me, her only daughter.

Mama was the strongest link in our small family. She was tough. She taught all of us to be tough. But, most of all, she taught us to take care of whatever we got our hands on. She was an excellent model of taking little and making much. Despite her impoverished beginning, when she died in 2001, Mama was worth half a million dollars in real estate and cash. She left that kind of legacy for my brother and me to share. I think she lived a remarkable life. The fabric of her character and its influence on me is consistently and intricately interwoven throughout my story.

-My Father-

My father did not acquire much formal education. He only attended school through the third grade. His life was consumed by work in the fields and a rapid spiral into adult activities. He grew up loving fast cars and fast women. He was dark skinned and handsome, with black, silky, wavy hair and a disarming smile. He also possessed a friendly personality—to a fault. Early on, he learned to live by his wits; gambling, hustling, and drinking alcohol became core to his existence. There was also a spiritual side to his life…of sorts. He grew up singing gospel music in quartets with his cousins and friends. Often he would travel from city to city singing at various church events. It was a love that he cherished until his death.

His two sisters, Ethel and Minnie Lee (nicknamed, Dolly), adored him and pampered him at every opportunity. His visits home to Texas were highlights in their lives for as long as he and they lived. Through him, I learned to love them, too. Their children are my friends and closest relatives to this very day.

My first memories of Daddy are from the days when he drove a taxi (his own car) between Safford and Fort Huachuca, Arizona, during the Second World War. Black soldiers, some of them members of the renowned Buffalo Soldiers, paid him to taxi them back and forth to enjoy recreational activities off-post. Buses were segregated, and time was scarce. Daddy made a ton of money—and blew it all. Maybe this was why Mama left him; I don't know. She only talked about the infidelity. What I do know is that she didn't leave her kids behind; instead, she took us with her.

When Mama moved to Tucson, Daddy moved there too. As we were growing up, we learned that he was the guy to go to when we needed a couple of bucks. And he was good for the carnival every year. He'd pick us up and treat us to a good time at least one night out of the year. Also, Daddy bought the bicycles for Christmas and my first Victrola record player. I guess you might say he was the "big ticket" guy.

Because his lifestyle still consisted of a good deal of drinking and carousing, Mama did not encourage too much stay-over time at Daddy's house. Besides, places like Sabino Alley, where he once lived, were not exactly safe abodes for anyone, let alone small children. Once, while living there, Daddy was shot five times in the stomach by his common-law wife. Mama's blood was typed to his for the transfusion that saved his life.

I was a source of great pride to my father. As a very young child, he allowed me to accompany him into bars and other scurrilous places. While he drank and argued politics with the soldiers, I would sit or stand on the barstool beside him and comb his wavy hair into "styles" of my own design. This was amusing to him and fun for me, a three-year-old. The men gave me money to buy bubble gum and candy. I enjoyed these special times. I was Daddy's little girl, and I knew it. Throughout his lifetime, I felt a duty to please my father as much or more than my mother. He counted on me. I was always in the spotlight as far as he was concerned. I was his "big brag." He kept up with my activities and told all of his friends about them.

During his years in Tucson, Daddy garnered the love and respect of many people. He worked at a carwash that was situated next to the courthouse in downtown Tucson. There was also a parking lot whose clients were the town's upper crust—lawyers, judges, and prominent city employees parked there, and my dad serviced their automobiles. He knew virtually everybody. His buddies gathered there daily for camaraderie. They laughed and lied in rhythmical alternating patterns day after day. For many, these meetings dispelled loneliness and despair that might otherwise have consumed them. These guys loved Daddy and looked forward to spending time with him.

He also loved sports, especially baseball. Daddy formed a baseball team of young black boys, many of them my and my brother's classmates. He proudly sponsored them in intra-mural games at local parks. They played their hearts out for "Carl." It was a love affair. In return, he bought them food and uniforms and offered fatherly counseling plus a little cash as needed. The Huckaby brothers— Billy, Clifton, and Willie—along with Veron Davis, Leland Brown, Marshall Bacon, Vernon Andrews, and many others whose names now escape me, faithfully met my dad for practice and games during baseball season. They hold fond memories of his enthusiasm and leadership.

Marriage was not something my father was good at. He married many times—how many, I'm just not sure. Frankly, I lost track after three. But his final marriage to Lillie Mae Goss was his most productive. "Mama Mae," as I called her, was ten years Daddy's senior. She was a solid, down-to-earth, Christian woman who took no nonsense. They were married for ten years. In that time, Daddy cleaned up his act: he stopped drinking and gambling, started going to church (in fact, he became a preacher), and started saving money instead of spending every dime. He also took interest in raising her two grandsons, Randy and Michael Sims. They thought of him as their father, calling him Daddy Carl. Daily involvement with them invigorated him. In many ways, taking care of the boys had redeeming value. It helped him quit his bad habits and gave him a greater sense of purpose.

Losing Lillie Mae was a severe blow to Daddy's forward thrust. When she died, a gradual decline in his own health and stamina slowly manifested itself. Five years later, my father died of diabetes and heart failure at age seventy-two. He did not know how to take care of himself, and I was too far away to help.

-My Brother-

Carl Jr. was always the child who few people really understood. He was a wiry, hyperactive boy who had an insatiable curiosity about things—especially mechanical things. He would take anything apart to see how it worked then put it back together again. For this, he was often labeled "destructive." He played with things with moving parts: wooden scooters (which he constructed from wooden crates or just lengths of two-by-fours nailed together with a long narrow handle and mobilized by metal skate wheels), yo-yos, bikes, and tin can walkers (made from large tin cans, turned upside down, to which he attached a length of wire or cord through holes punched on each side with an ice pick). When I played with him, we clattered noisily down the dirt sidewalk perched atop our walkers, holding on to the wires to keep us from falling as we stepped.

Junior also loved to attach thread to the legs of june bugs, large green beetles with wide wings that flew about in plentiful numbers in the summer. He and his friends captured them, tied them up, and held contests to see whose bug could fly highest and farthest. A restless child, Junior nervously drummed on everything he touched—a habit that got him into hot water more than a few times at the dinner table.

In school, he was not considered a scholar, though he never failed a grade either. He had a speech impediment that I've come to know as cluttered speech, which made him difficult to understand when he spoke. People would laugh at him and tell him, "Boy, slow down, I can't understand a word you said!"

There were no speech therapists available to diagnose and treat his disability, so Carl grew up with the stigma of being one who couldn't talk well. He was also dyslexic; therefore, he couldn't read or spell well either. It doesn't take a very smart person to imagine how frustrating this must have been for a young child.

Junior figured out very early that having money made him equal to just about everybody else. He pursued several lucrative business enterprises from the time he was very young: he shined shoes at the Greyhound bus station, threw the daily newspaper on a large route of prominent homes, and sold everything from comic books to contraband telephone hookups. He once got in serious trouble when he swiped some cable and phone receivers from the telephone company's storage lot and "hooked up" all of his friends within a two-mile radius to telephone lines. He set up the whole network and operated it out of a shed that was located in our backyard. We didn't have a phone, but *he* did! Yes, he was an enterprising kid, to say the least!

He could con me into doing a lot of his work. I folded newspapers at five o'clock in the morning just to be called his super girl. And I ironed stiffly starched, wet Levi denim jeans for the promise of a quarter. I was a big sucker sister whom he shamelessly took advantage of!

Most of all, Junior loved things with motors, like cars. He was very talented at working on them and fixing them for his friends. Our house was always the center for gatherings of the town's grease monkeys (that's what we called shade tree mechanics in those days). Some of them, like Donald Lander, were very cute. I liked that! Unfortunately, they, like my brother, never paid me any attention.

As to our relationship, I cannot say that it has always been a close one. This is largely due to the breakup of our home while we were both young. When we were kids, we competed with each other for our parents' attention, both of us winning for opposite reasons. By the time we might have bonded, Junior had moved out of our home to the streets. He left when he was fifteen years old, and he never came back. When life got too hard, he quit school to join the military.

After serving in the U.S. Navy, he made his home in Northern California, rarely traveling south for visits. For a time, he successfully pursued family life and business ownership. In fact, at one point, he owned two large gasoline stations with garages. Then everything fell apart. There was divorce, loss of the stations, and loss of his home. Humpty Dumpty never was put together again.

Today, we cling to a fragile sibling relationship, and that fragility is exacerbated by distance and time. With our parents gone, we try to hold on to each other. We are often surprised at how similar we are at the core. But, we shouldn't be surprised at all, for no matter how far away we have traveled or how diverse our experiences have been, we both were shaped by Tucson, our parents, the community, and Dunbar school.

-"Big Mama"-

The first smell that I can remember was that of banana pudding, my Big Mama's banana pudding. I was barely two years old when my grandmother and Papa (my grandfather) moved to Safford, Arizona, where my mother and father had settled to pick cotton for a while. Mama was Papa's youngest child from a previous marriage. There were seven children, altogether, including five stepchildren who belonged to Big Mama.

He never let her get too far from his view, especially since her two children were his only grandchildren. Though she was technically my stepgrandmother, Big Mama could not have loved a child more than she loved me. When I was still very young, she often kept me while my parents worked. Her lap was generous, plump, and warm. She often held me close to her warm bosom and rocked me to sleep. Her rocking was the only rocking that I recall. Back and forth, back and forth, she rocked me in her old, creaky, rocking chair on the front porch of their tiny wooden framed home. Big Mama dipped snuff— all day, every day. Her soft humming while we rocked was interrupted by an occasional pause in which she picked up her spit can from the floor beside the chair and spat brown juices.

When she knew I would be there, Big Mama would make a banana pudding, not from Jell-O Pudding and Pie Filling; hers was from scratch: fresh eggs; sugar; and creamy, canned, evaporated milk enhanced with vanilla extract. A spoonful of Big Mama's banana pudding was, and still is, to me, synonymous with a spoonful of love.

-"Papa"-

My grandfather, Roger Williams, was a character, the likes of which could fill an entire book. A jocular fellow, he was never without female companionship. You had to like him. He was a tall, wiry, funny man who could always think of a joke that paralleled any situation. He enjoyed tickling me and my brother under our arms and down our sides. To watch us writhe in laughter was his ultimate pleasure. It made him laugh loudly too. We loved being around him. When my parents separated, Mom and we two kids moved to Tucson. Papa soon followed, without Big Mama. I never knew what happened. I've heard many theories. After his marriage to Big Mama ended, and he had relocated to Tucson, he was married once more to another woman, who also divorced him.

After moving to Tucson, my brother and I often stayed for days with Papa during his bachelor years in his small, tin-shack-of-a-home on Tyndall Avenue, which he heated with a smoky coal oil heater ventilated with a metal pipe that went straight up through the roof. The fumes were sometimes suffocating, but we were kept warm. My brother and I slept with Papa on a large cot. I slept in the middle and usually wet the bed. Papa never made a big issue of it, although my brother sure did. Papa just hung the wet bedding out on the line, and we slept on it the next night, the smell notwithstanding. There was no washing machine. Laundry was done in a metal washtub with scalding hot water that was heated on that coal oil stove. Hot water, a rub board, and a bar of lye soap got the job done.

At daybreak, Papa would rise ahead of us kids, throw on a pair of khaki pants, and tuck a cup towel around his waist. He would then stoke up the coal oil cook stove and produce the tastiest hot cakes, homemade biscuits, and slab bacon one could ever hope to eat. He taught us to love the taste of sweet, thick sorghum syrup, warmed and poured over two or three pancakes topped by mounds of butter, which was also slathered in between.

At night, dinner was likely to consist of a tall glass of buttermilk into which fresh cornbread was crumbled. Two heaping tablespoonfuls of sugar stirred into the mixture made for delicious eating.

All the while he was cooking, sweeping, or hanging up wet bedding, Papa would either whistle or hum some sort of church song. He was almost never silent. The guy loved to talk, and he could tell story after story for hours on end. Whenever he rose to testify in church, my brother and I would slump down in the pew and position ourselves for a long snooze. His life was not a long one (he died at age fifty), but it seemed that he had an awful lot to be grateful for if one believed his voluminous testimonies.

One of the worst whuppin's I ever got was due to my behavior in church while Papa was leading a congregational hymn. He had a particularly large Adam's apple—which we kids called his goozle—that went up and down in a pronounced pattern whenever he sang. On a certain Sunday night, this picture was just too much for my impish brother to take in without giggling. He was never happy, it seemed, until he got me giggling with him; we knew full well that we would both be treading on dangerous waters in the church house setting. Nevertheless, with his constant poking and pointing, my tickle cup ran over too, and I couldn't help snickering. Soon it was louder than either of us could control, and in short order we were both hauled out of the sanctuary by our collars and pounded by our stepfather, Deacon Matthew Hill. He was a no-nonsense kind of guy who would wallop either of us at the drop of a hat when we misbehaved. Somehow, Papa's Adam's apple was never so funny after that.

During his lifetime, wherever we went, Papa followed us. Often this was from cotton patch to cotton patch. He was an incredibly hard worker. It was nothing for Papa and his baby daughter, my mother, Copply, or Hunk as the family called her to pick a thousand pounds of cotton a day between them. And just as Hunk was a source of pride to Papa, he was her shelter against any storm. She adored and depended on him to protect her and us kids from all harm. He owned a shotgun, and she knew he would shoot it if he had to.

After her separation from my father, in spite of her remarriage, Papa was always the main man in Mama's life. While he lived, no man dared take advantage of her. His early death, from tuberculosis, caught her quite off guard. It was the only time I ever saw her weep. It was also the only time I witnessed her neediness. I was ten. We clung to each other for comfort. I don't remember another such time. Papa, her rock, was gone. I'm not sure she ever got over losing him.

As for me, I went to the funeral, but I would not look at my Papa's dead body. I still remember him as I last saw him: dressed up in his tan-colored Sunday suit, accented by a black shirt and brown tie, hat cocked to the side of his head, leaning against his old Dodge sedan laughing heartily, his goozle going up and down.

-Earlee and Charles Jackson-

My other Big Mama, my maternal grandmother, came into my life when I was about five years old. She was the birth mother that Mama had not lived with since early childhood. Although she and her second husband, Mr. Charlie, as we called him, lived in town and attended our same church, we did not spend a lot of time with them while we were growing up. My grandmother believed in paying tithes to the church, and she faithfully and generously gave one-tenth of whatever she earned every Sunday in the offering.

In addition to being a generous tither, Big Mama Earlee was a very attractive woman who learned to powder and perfume her body as a means of getting positive attention—especially at church, where everyone remarked about how good she smelled and looked. She carried this behavior to extremes at times. For example, she dressed in a starched and ironed nurse's uniform—cap, cape, shoes, white stockings, and all—when she was going to work to scrub floors and clean toilets in the private homes of white folks. She usually softly sang her favorite church song while she scrubbed, hung out clothes, or ironed: "This little light of mine, I'm gonna let it shine, let it shine, let it shine, let it shine!"

Big Mama Earlee was a very proud individual, and she displayed her pride in different aspects of her life as well as in her personal demeanor. Her small, adobe stucco house on South Park Avenue was a showpiece. It was whitewashed every other year, and her oval, green lawn, lined with gleaming white rocks and beautiful red and yellow rose bushes, captured the attention of passersby. She was artistic, frequently painting the inside of her four-room home by herself. She etched little pillows of clouds out of white putty for special accent over a blue ceiling in the bedroom. And her delicious seven-layered banana cake was the most sought-after prize at any of the church's fundraising events.

After living for many years in Tucson, these aging grandparents of mine ended up moving to Los Angeles, living in a cramped two-room rented house around the corner from Mama. Their first move had been to the Bay area where Aunt Rosetta lived, but, for reasons that I don't know, that didn't work out so well, so they moved to Southern

California. By then, my grandmother had become a victim of what appeared to be Alzheimer's disease, though there was never a clear diagnosis of this. Perhaps, judging from the behavior that I observed, she was simply deeply depressed. She stopped caring about her appearance and her hygiene. It was hard to get her to even pull up her stockings or tie her shoes. She was very lonely; she had no friends with whom to communicate in this busy, impersonal, new environment.

It was difficult for me, at age twenty-one, to witness the changes in her. Believing that I could somehow lift her spirits with some new clothes to wear, I spent most of my first paycheck from my teaching job buying new dresses, underwear, and stockings for my grandmother. She graciously accepted them, but they made little or no difference in her daily behavior. Sadly, she died from an aneurysm when she was sixty years old. Her husband, who was twenty years her senior, outlived her by eight years.

-"Mr. Hill"-

Mama's remarriage thrust my brother and me into a life cycle that was fraught with uncertainty and a good deal of fear. Her new husband, Matthew Hill—Mr. Hill, as Junior and I always called him—could be volatile. He was known for his temper. He once beat up a fellow deacon right on the church grounds for saying something he didn't like about his uncle, Reverend Sam Dabner. He was undereducated and also chronically ill with severe diabetes, which he'd had since he was a child growing up in Louisiana. He wore his frustrations, born out of insecurity and the inability to get a firm grip on life—especially economically—on his sleeve. It took very little to set him off. Once he became angry, he didn't seem to be able to control his emotions. He would rant on and on loudly at my mother or in the act of scolding us kids. I guess you could say we were afraid of him when he got into those moods, but we always had Mama as a buffer, and we knew he would not seriously hurt us. Now, I don't mean that he wouldn't wallop us; oh yes, he would. He kept his belt handy for that purpose. He even had a razor strap and ironing cords that we felt profoundly on occasions. We knew what it was like to have large welts imprinted on our backs and legs that turned to dark bruises and lasted for a long time. Was he a child-abuser? To this day, I don't think so.

It was customary within our race, in those days, to discipline children harshly. The external social context was both racist and unforgiving, making it a dangerous place in which to raise children without internalized boundaries and limits. Everybody I knew got whuppin's. Most often, it was a means of parental control that both taught in-group morals and values and protected us from inadvertent behavioral acts that could be lethal if perpetrated in that outside social context. Nobody died from these extreme disciplinary measures, although I suspect all of us were scarred both outwardly and inwardly. Mr. Hill and other parents raised us as they themselves had been raised. On the positive side, few of us went to jail for committing crimes in the community, and most of us grew up to be respectful, responsible adults.

For Mama, the picture was more complex: her new husband just could not stay employed. He had minimal skills to begin with, usually washing dishes, cleaning commercial buildings, or doing yard work. The pay was always low. Additionally, he would invariably have a diabetic seizure in the midst of some job and get fired. Once, he was arrested for sitting down under a shade tree on his way home from work. He had felt a seizure coming on. He was weak and incoherent when the police arrived. They automatically assumed he was a "drunk Negro" and carried him off to jail, though there was no evidence of alcohol. It was enough to make a man mad. He was humiliated beyond words. Mr. Hill, after all, had a reputation among church folk as being a fiery deacon who prayed fervently and loudly during services, usually until someone who was overcome by the spirit "shouted." Sometimes the loud, emotional screaming was accompanied by the shouter flailing about in the aisles or in the pews. Ushers in uniforms were kept busy fanning people with paper fans to control these outbursts. Sometimes the shouters were physically carried outside until they recovered; then they would return for the rest of the service. (Later, as a teenager, I'd often sneak away from BYPU at Mt. Calvary Baptist Church, which I had joined, and went with other kids to peek into the windows of the Holiness Church near Dunbar to watch entire congregations engaging in this "shouting" behavior. Additionally, they would beat tambourines and drums and dance wildly about the sanctuary. I can't say today with any accuracy what the spiritual impact of these observations was on me. At minimum, I can truly say it was moving to be absorbed in the rhythm of these episodes, but for us thrill-seeking teens with nothing better to do, being spectators was mostly entertainment.)

Mr. Hill also sang very well. I often sang with him while traveling to or from church in our old car, a 1929 Ford convertible, which our family and friends fondly called, "B-29." The nickname was boldly painted in large white letters on both sides of the hood. He was a proud man about such things as these. It hurt him to have been arrested.

The relationship between Mama and my stepfather became very fragile after Papa died. Mama had no back up. She was not on particularly good terms with Rev. Dabner nor was she close to any of her other in-laws and not really close to her birth mother and stepfather, who were now living in town. She felt pretty much alone in handling her marital situation. Things eventually deteriorated to the level of spousal violence. When he couldn't out-argue her, Mr. Hill would take to physically assaulting my mother. He would strike her with a hard fist in the face and even try to whip her with his belt as he would whip one of us kids. Mama didn't stand still and take it; neither did she resort to tears and submission; she would pick up something— anything—and strike back as hard as she could.

Observing these frequent episodes was terrifying to me. My brother would jump in to defend his mother if he was at home when it started. Then he would become a target of Mr. Hill's rage, too. There was screaming and running in and out of the house by all involved. Neighbors would come out of their houses to watch the melee. It was utterly embarrassing to me.

Truthfully, I often silently sided with my stepfather. Mama had kind of an acid tongue. Once she started in on you, she wouldn't quit until she had stripped away every ounce of resistance in your body. She would go on and on, bringing up every nuance of the issue she was upset about, recalling infinite details of the history of your past actions or wrongdoings. She just wouldn't let go. With us kids, she could set us down on the couch and make us listen until she was darned well through. But this tactic only exacerbated the seething nature of Mr. Hill's temperament. His fuse was very short. Within a few minutes, he would come out swinging. I dreaded those fights. How I would wish Mama could have just shut up a few minutes earlier. As young as I was, I could see that this pattern of communication was way off course, but I felt powerless to intervene. Kids were to be seen, not heard in those days. So I suffered in silence, caught between the only two people I loved and trusted.

Mama had a tragic automobile accident in the midst of these turbulent times. She had begun purchasing two cans of beer on her way home from work and drinking them to relax before Mr. Hill got home from his work, when he was employed.

One day, she had left home late en route to pick him up from his job at McDonnell-Douglas Aircraft Company. It was a bit of a journey from our house, so she had to hurry. She definitely didn't want to keep him waiting. That would not have been good. The route took her along a Farm-to-Market (FM) road through a rural area on the outskirts of the city. It was a narrow, two-lane, tree-lined road. While driving at the maximum speed limit, Mama approached a yellow school bus and proceeded to pass the small bus, which had stopped to drop off a student. Just as she went around the bus, a small, blond-haired girl dashed into her path to cross the street to where her mother stood waiting. A metal knob from the broken off rear view mirror on the passenger's side of Mama's car struck the child and tore one of her eyes out of its socket. Stunned, Mama skidded to a stop several yards away and sat there for a few minutes. She was numb with shock. Crowds gathered around the child and around her car. She didn't get out of her car. It was not a pretty picture. She was gripped with fear.

Fortunately, the child was not killed. She suffered a concussion, and, of course, sadly, lost her little eye. Mama was charged with failure to stop for a school bus and had to hire a lawyer to defend her in court from a potentially severe sentence. There was no mention of suspicion of use of alcohol. Mama's attorney discovered a loophole in the state law regarding the requirement to stop when school bus lights flashed, and her case was dismissed with a fine.

Newspapers and radio broadcasts carried details of the incident.

We had acquired a phone by then, and our number was listed in the phone book. Many an anonymous threatening telephone call came to our house for weeks. Mama handled the situation well. Though burdened by the guilt of what she had done, she went on about her life, doing what she had to do. Looking back, I'm sure she felt very remorseful and lonely during those stressful weeks and months that followed the accident. It hurt all of us to think how this beautiful little girl would be disfigured for the rest of her life. I felt scared, too. What could happen to my Mama? For years afterward, she saved the newspaper clippings. Then, one day, she just threw them away. I guess she finally forgave herself. I rarely heard her mention the incident after that.

When she finally had had enough of the endless anguish over insufficient money and the arguing and physical fighting that became more frequent, Mama made the decision to leave her marriage. A wonderful white woman whom she had met at the YWCA, where she worked, and in whom she had confided, had quite unexpectedly handed her an envelope containing two hundred dollars one day. She'd admonished her not to open it until she got home. Unable to bear the suspense, Mama had opened the envelope in the grocery store that she stopped at en route to our house. She was stunned.

A note that was enclosed read: "Copply, please take care of yourself, and always trust in God. He will give you direction and light your path."

Tears fell from Mama's eyes as she clutched the contents of the letter. She had the answer she had sought in her prayers.

One day shortly after that, while Mr. Hill was at work, Mama packed everything she could into the family's 1950 Ford Sedan and headed for the Interstate 10 Highway; she was on her way to California! She had a cousin there, living someplace in Los Angeles. She would find her. That was all she knew. She arranged for me to stay with my father until she could get settled. Junior had moved out of the house by this point and was living with friends he had found near Meyers Street. It was not the best environment for a teenage boy, but he was determined to stay away from home. With the two of us out of the house, and in relatively safe places, Mama left Tucson to find a better life elsewhere. She wrote letters to me and my grandparents several times each month. In them, she often enclosed money for me and some for my grandparents to help with my care. She frequently told me how much she loved and missed me and assured me that she was doing all she could to get situated in a place where I could join her.

※

-Reflections-

Though I wouldn't want to relive any of the episodes or trauma and drama that characterized our home life, I, nonetheless, believe that I learned to live through tough times with valor during those years. I internalized the phrase, "Never let 'em see you sweat." I've had to use that attitude more than a little in my lifetime. Back then it meant "Hold your head up, don't look down." "Be strong, keep on walking."

That's what my neighbors would tell me in the days after they had witnessed the beatings and commotion around my home. They always encouraged me to strive toward a better day—to keep a positive focus, because I was going to "be somebody" someday. These positive words were often augmented by gifts of a few extra dollars, something pretty to wear, a hairdo, or just time and a sandwich in my neighbors' more peaceful homes. I grew up feeling that I was special to a few people who knew my story and cared about where I was headed. I've never wanted to disappoint these precious individuals. It is for their memory that I continue to reach for higher heights—that I continue to try to learn and grow.

Carl Jr. and I also learned the intangible value and importance of work in that tumultuous home of ours. We were given chores and daily responsibilities, tasks, to do. There were both quality-of-performance standards and deadlines for completion. Usually it was, "Have these things done by the time I get home from work."

Junior and I knew exactly what those words meant. We were to do the housecleaning, yard cleaning, laundry, and any other assignments as if an adult were doing them; Mama had no tolerance for mediocrity when it came to labor. We would get a good whuppin' if we slacked off and played all day instead of doing our work. On his mean-big-brother days, Junior would lock me out of the house until just before time for Mama to return. I had to sweat mightily to finish my chores, but I seldom got the dreaded punishment for non-completion.

I learned to wash snow-white sheets and shirts, hang clothes perfectly on the clothesline out back, and iron to perfection. Our house reeked of Lysol and Pine-Sol. We cleaned it regularly and thoroughly. I even started my own little ironing business. I ironed clothes for other people and earned my own money. This was my initiation into the first levels of independence and self-reliance. I had money to buy my own clothes and shoes that I liked. It was powerful stuff.

Sometimes I had more money than good sense—like the time when, at age thirteen, I bought a pink, tight-fitting, sleeveless, low-cut, rhinestone-decorated dress with deep splits on the sides to wear to Easter Sunday church services. Mama was not amused. She made me take it right back to Lerner's Department Store where I had bought it. I thought she was just being mean, so to show my rebellion, I exchanged the dress for an ugly, long, gray, uniform-looking, taffeta dress that had a big collar, sleeves, and buttons up to the neck. It was really ugly. Well, the bottom line was that it was my only dressy dress, so, like it or not, I had to wear it every Sunday for months.

My independence grew over time, and I learned to spend money more wisely, but the roots of that wisdom were planted in that very home environment. I've never regretted learning to discern between spending to impress others and spending for what I truly needed. A simple lesson in economics (and taste) has gone a long way. Many of my best clothes were ones that were handed down from the young, white women who lived at the Y. They were usually well cared for and stylish enough for me. Those secondhand gifts helped out a lot. I felt very appreciative. No one, except me, knew they were not new when I wore them.

To this day, I search through used clothing and furniture stores looking for items I need that have been gently used before I purchase new ones. I know, from experience, that things don't have to be new to be good.

We didn't have a lot of store-bought toys or books. Mama frequently brought home old copies of the *Reader's Digest*, which was the source of much of my recreational reading. I found inspiring stories in it that made me feel that my life was not so bad after all; there were people all over the world with worse problems. Occasionally, we would get a *Chicago Defender* from a salesperson passing through our neighborhood. Mama avidly read news about black people who were living far from Tucson. None of the local media carried stories about Negroes who were doing positive things—those things were not newsworthy it seemed. Only black crime or sports-related triumphs made the news. The athletic feats of Larry Doby, Roy Campanella, and Satchel Paige were regularly featured in the Sports section of our newspapers. This was because the Cleveland Indians Baseball Team held winter practice in Tucson and the spotlight was always on those particular sports stars. It was a treat to read a *Defender* or an *Ebony* magazine. Working on a large picture puzzle was another activity that could take days and weeks to complete. It taught us patience and perseverance. Sticking with such an arduous activity culminated in feelings of great satisfaction and had the secondary benefit of keeping our hands busy when we weren't engaged in work. Believe me, we had no use for the words, "I'm bored."

I don't remember anything about Greenville, Texas, my birthplace, until I became twelve years old and began returning there every summer for several years with my parents for a visit with my cousins and aunts on Daddy's side. I got to spend a couple of weeks every year with them while Mama and my stepfather traveled on to Louisiana to visit his parents and siblings. Those were some of the happiest times of my life. Although I loved both of Daddy's sisters, I adored my Aunt Dolly, who doted on me by kissing and hugging me a lot. She also cooked many of my favorite foods—fried chicken, greens with ham hocks, fried corn, and sweet potato pies—whenever I visited with her and her six kids.

My girl cousins, Louise, Lottie Mae, Kathlean, and Joyce

Williams were like the sisters I never had. We loved doing "girly" things together: straightening and curling each others' hair, trading clothes to wear out at night, applying makeup to each others' faces (once we were out of Aunt Dolly's sight), dancing at the little neighborhood juke joint where other teens hung out, and talking about boys in whispers under the covers for hours after we returned home from an outing. We all slept in the same bed, some at the head, some at the foot, but being together was the most important part.

When I visited them, I learned a lot of domestic skills from them, too. We washed clothes and bedding in a big iron pot that sat on a bed of hot coals and twigs in the backyard. The water was boiling hot. We had to lift the garments out of the pot with sticks and transfer them to a tub where we rubbed them on a metal rubboard to get them sparkling clean and free of stains. We used large chunks of homemade lye soap for detergent. We then transferred the clean clothes and sheets to another large metal tub that contained cold water for rinsing. For white things, we used "bluing" in the final rinse. This was a dark blue commercial solution that came in a bottle, which, when dissolved in the water, made the fabrics snow-white. We worked as a team to accomplish the laundering, all the way from retrieving the laundry from the boiling pot to wringing out each piece and clipping it to the long clotheslines that were made of thick rope strung along tall, wooden poles that were split at the top to hold the rope and stuck in the ground to hold them and the clothes up to the sun. Once the laundry was dry, we took each piece down, folded everything neatly, and got prepared for the next day's task of ironing them by sprinkling the clothes with water from a wash pan, rolling them up tightly, and placing them in a pillow slip. Work like this consumed most of our days. After a little rest and a routine of taking turns bathing in a large, #2 tin bathtub, we were glad to anticipate a few hours of frivolous, carefree recreation.

What I remember just as vividly from those visits was the sign I saw above and across Main Street in downtown Greenville. In bold letters it said:

GREENVILLE, WELCOME

Then, on each side of the city's name there were some additional words. One side said:

THE BLACKEST LAND

The other side said:

THE WHITEST PEOPLE

I was stunned. I was furious! It was the wrong metaphor, especially for those times. I don't think it ever was meant to be taken as literally as it was taken, but what it was intended to mean (fertile black soil, really nice people) was lost in the impact of unexplained words in the context of an oppressed setting for black residents of the city.

Those of us who were black translated that sign to mean something very ugly and racist. In fact, folklore about the sign insists that there was a sub-message that was to be understood. That message was passed along in the oral history of the region. It went like this:

Nigger, if you can read, RUN! If you can't read, RUN anyway.

Some people still believe that these words were scripted on another actual sign nearby, but others deny it. I'm not sure what is true; there are so many different accounts about the origin of this saying, including one account that places such a sign in a town near Greenville but close enough to connect the dots, in many people's opinion, to what seemed to be inferred by the big sign across Main Street. What is clear is that the perceived aim of signs such as these (and even rumors about them) was intimidation. After all, historically, there had been numerous documented cases of brutal beatings and lynchings perpetrated against blacks, particularly black males, in Greenville, Texas. Daddy once showed me a newspaper article that had been handed down to him by his father, Cash Robinson. It contained gruesome photographs and a lead story about the mob beating of a man named Ted Smith in the summer of 1908 for allegedly assaulting a fourteen-year-old white girl near a railroad track. Although Daddy said that the accused vehemently denied the charge against him, stating repeatedly that he was nowhere near where the assault had taken place, Smith was beaten by a mob of angry white men until he was unconscious and then burned to death in the Greenville town square while hundreds of whites watched. My eyes popped out wide with disbelief as Daddy told that story.

Memories like this one have fed the folklore about Greenville for years. Folklore about the sign is so well disseminated that when someone begins, "the blackest land," black people across America, whether they've seen the sign or not, can finish the rest.

Many years later, the sign in Greenville was taken down—forced down by political pressure exerted by more enlightened white and black people who didn't want the stigma of racism to continue to affect life in Greenville and its political and economic potential. The continuing negative perception conveyed by that sign was keeping the city from realizing its destiny.

Today, it is a thriving city that has grown up on the impetus of government and private industrial developments. Major manufacturing and military plants dot the landscape of the once depressed little town that was crippled by its image. Things were very much black and white in that little East Texas town where I was born; water fountains were labeled *Colored* and *White*, though they were located side by side; and we still had to step off the sidewalk when we encountered a white person coming our way in order to let them pass well apart from us. My cousins yanked me many a time to make me comply with these ridiculous, racist customs. I hated them. My aunt couldn't even try on hats and dresses that she bought. It wasn't allowed back then. Time, courts, and education have since converged to bring about needed change.

Part II

School and Community Life

No man who continues to add something to the material, intellectual and moral well-being of the place in which he lives is left long without reward.

—Booker T. Washington

My Teachers

-Miss Shaw-

Miss Shaw, my first teacher, was a large, buxom, dark-skinned woman with really short black hair, who loved children. She cared for several preschoolers every day in Miss Shaw's Nursery School while their parents worked. My brother, Carl Jr., was old enough to attend the public school for colored children, Dunbar Elementary, but I was too young. I had to go to nursery school while my mother, who was starting over in a brand-new world, worked as a waitress at the Studio Patio, a local restaurant that catered to tourists. Having Miss Shaw care for me while she worked helped make that transition easier.

It was here that I was first read to, that I heard the first nursery rhymes: "Hey Diddle Diddle," "Mistress Mary, Quite Contrary," "Humpty Dumpty," "The Gingerbread Man," "Hansel and Gretel," and other classics. Fairy tales came alive when Miss Shaw read them. She would open her big eyes wide, feigning surprise and shock at different intervals in a story and creating suspense and wonderment as she read to us. I cried when Hansel and Gretel were lost in the forest and couldn't find their way home. And that mean old witch—aagh! Rapunzel's long tresses were so beautiful in the pictures; I always wished my own hair could grow that long. Miss Shaw had a soothing contralto voice that she used to sing the lullabies that put us to sleep for afternoon naps, lullabies I would sing to my own babies many years later and later still to my grandbabies.

She, too, made vanilla and banana puddings for treats and sat down with us to eat them. I learned to say "please" and "thank you" as well as "excuse me" and "I'm sorry"—phrases that have served me well throughout my life.

Sharing was a big thing in Shaw's Nursery School. Most of us had few toys at home, so learning to share toys we liked with others was not easy to master. I especially liked playing house in the corner play center that had a toy iron and ironing board and a table with four small chairs. There was also a miniature wooden cook stove, a little broom, and some small pots and doll dishes. All the skills of good housekeeping could be learned and practiced right there. I loved to pretend that I was mother to three or four baldheaded dolls and a couple of worn out teddy bears. J. L. Washington was always willing to play the daddy role. He washed clothes, baked, and swept floors in the playhouse more than I did; I mostly rocked the babies. Funny how I remember *that*. I barely remember what J. L. looked like now, but he was my favorite "husband" when I was four.

Getting to Shaw's Nursery School was not always a safe journey from Dunbar, the elementary school where Mama dropped us both off. My brother was responsible for walking me the rest of the distance to nursery school before his classes started. Once he had me crawl under four sets of train cars stopped on the tracks that crossed Main Street near the school. Patience was not Junior's strong suit. He wanted to have time left over when he got back to school to play a little ball with his friends before the bell rang signaling that it was time to go inside to classrooms.

Just as we got midway through the last set of tracks, there was a sudden lurch, and the train started slowly moving forward. I was petrified! Realizing imminent danger, he yelled at me and tugged my paralyzed body to safety on the other side. I've often chided him about the story he would have told Mom had the worst happened. Nothing he could have said would have saved him from death at her hand.

-Morgan Maxwell-

If ever I believed in giants, I believed that Morgan Maxwell, Dunbar's ambitious principal, was one of them. Technically, he was only about five foot nine, but he was a giant of a man in so many other ways. Mr. Maxwell ("Eagle Eyes" as he was called behind his back by us students) "took no prisoners" when it came to his school.

During the height of the Jim Crow era, he eloquently and fiercely fought for better books, better facilities, and better teachers. He spent his summers traveling to the Midwest (Kansas, Illinois, and Indiana) to recruit the best black teachers he could find. Speaking impeccable English and carrying a heavy, sincere burden in his heart for the future of the eight hundred or so black kids that populated classrooms in his Dunbar School, Mr. Maxwell soldiered steadfastly and valiantly, winning many a battle. We graduates and near-graduates will always owe a huge debt to him.

Morgan Maxwell personified the word *leader*. His was the face of triumph. Although our books were secondhand ones handed down from white schools in the district when they were either obsolete or too worn for their students' use), and though we had few new technologies of that day such as typewriters, televisions, or radios, we were, nonetheless, fed a constant diet of praise. We were not taught to feel sorry for ourselves as victims of an unfair system. Morgan Maxwell assaulted feelings of inferiority with constant positive verbiage. He bragged *on* us and *to* us: "You are the finest boys and girls in the world." He repeated this theme daily until we believed it.

We never felt second-class—not at Dunbar. We were exposed to the cultures of many people through the arts. We often boarded school buses to attend symphony concerts, operas and plays at the University of Arizona. It was through these experiences, fostered largely by our school's leader, that our aspirations were allowed to soar. In the hallway outside the main office, a banner bearing this slogan hung for as long as I can remember: "Have a star, and try to reach its height. All things are possible to the courageous." It was signed by Marian Anderson, the renowned operatic contralto of her day. Mr. Maxwell believed that. I came to believe it, too. "Be the best," he told us; "Be the best!"

-Miss Carter-

By the time I was six, I, too, could attend Dunbar. It was there where, as a first grader in Mrs. Carter's class, I learned to read for myself—all about Dick, Jane, Sally, Puff, and Spot. It was the dawning of a brand-new world! All of the reading to me that Mama and Miss

Shaw had done helped to make me ready to read words and formulate meanings very easily.

Miss Carter was a short, demure woman of somewhat stocky build. Her quiet, gentle demeanor was perfect for fostering and nurturing my earliest eager efforts to read whole books on my own. I was anxious to learn everything in my new school.

-The McHenry Sisters-

When I was about seven years old, my stepfather, Matthew Hill, was hired as a handyman for a well-known dairy, Shamrock Dairy, which was located just outside the boundary line of Tucson's city limits in a rural area. We actually moved to the dairy and lived in one of the houses provided for employees. It was the nicest house I had lived in up to that point. There were two bedrooms, a kitchen large enough for a table and chairs, and a nice bathroom with a tub and shower. We also had a yard with grass where I often played with my dolls. I could safely ride my bicycle on the dirt road just outside our fence. I really liked it there! Although it was a distance to drive, we could still go into town occasionally on Sundays to visit with friends and attend church.

Because we lived there at the dairy, I did not attend Dunbar for part of the second grade. Instead, we were schooled in a retired boxcar that had been converted into two classrooms. The "school" sat on a defunct track in the train stop near the dairy, known as Jaynes' Station. The McHenrys, two dedicated spinster sisters taught the classes, which were divided into the little kids and the big kids. It was the first time I had been taught by white teachers and my first experience with integration. Altogether, there couldn't have been more than two dozen students in the area who needed a school, so, in spite of the state's segregation policy, it was not economically feasible to separate the races there.

My passion for learning was awakened in that small setting. The slender, middle-aged teachers, who were Quakers, used flannel boards and colorful felt cutouts to teach us reading through storytelling, mostly about biblical characters. We learned about David and the mean giant, Goliath. How Saul became Paul on the road to

Damascus was vividly explained, as the teacher moved the characters from bottom to top of the large flannel board.

Best of all, I often got to retell the stories, manipulating the pieces and embellishing the facts. It was an excellent way to check students' comprehension and recall of story details. I wonder if they knew that's what they were doing. They were naturally good teachers who knew how to get children to learn and to enjoy it along the way. Having so few pupils in the classroom, they were able to be both flexible and consistent. Their deliberate, measured approach to instruction allowed me time to understand what I was being taught in small chunks. I was a good reader, but I had lots of trouble memorizing arithmetic facts. It was a long time before I finally had to confront this learning disability, but one day, years later, it caught up with me. That's another story.

The White family children (that was their last name) were the only other black children in attendance at the school as I recall. Their father worked for the railroad. There were three or four of them across the grades. One day, Andrew, the eldest, accidentally swallowed some caustic substance at home that nearly killed him. Today, he is a successful recording artist with a melodic singing voice. Seeing him at a recent Dunbar school reunion, in the prime of his life, looking great and doing so well, was the highlight of the reunion for me. All of us eventually moved back to Tucson and reentered the segregated school system.

Prior to moving back, my stepfather lost his job at the dairy, and we moved a few miles farther west to a small town called, Marana, where the main industry was cotton picking. Papa joined us there. All of us—Papa, my parents, Junior, and I—lived in one room behind the small café that exclusively served black clientele. It was operated by a Reverend Baker, whose first name I never knew. The room we lived in had no running water, so the bathroom was either in the café or there was a slop jar to be used at night. We kids and Papa slept on surplus army cots. There was a single bed for Mama and Mr. Hill, but there was no privacy for anyone.

Everyday during the week, a school bus picked the children of workers up and transported us to a one-room school house where Mr. Maxwell's wife, Mrs. Kathryn Maxwell, was the teacher. How this brave, talented, and brilliant woman skillfully taught over three dozen students ranging in age from seven to fifteen all by herself, I'll never know! She did what had to be done with seeming finesse. I remember being tutored as a young pupil by older students and following strict rules set down by Mrs. Maxwell about talking and playing during class time. She was firm, yet friendly. I enjoyed school work and tried hard to please her. Educational and recreational materials were scarce, but she used the chalkboard and whatever else she had effectively. We were kept busy working and learning. Her dedication paralleled that of her husband. Such an angel she was!

On Saturdays, Junior and I had to work at picking cotton in the fields with our parents and Papa. I gathered balls of soft, white, cotton from hardened petals with sharp edges that opened wide to expose the cotton. They grew on stalks from low and high bushes, set in rows that extended for what seemed like miles as we walked in irrigation ditches and picked from one end to the other. More often than not, the bushes were over my head, and I couldn't see where the end was. To reach the low branches, Papa and Mama often crawled on their knees for long distances pulling heavy sacks that were held over their backs by wide sturdy straps and that clung heavily, like long, thick snakes to the ground. I placed the cotton I picked into a short burlap sack which was securely tied across my shoulders with a string made of rags. When it was full, I'd empty the sack into Papa's or Mama's long, white canvas sack, and we would continue picking side by side until they either reached the end of their rows or stopped to carry their full sacks to the scales to be weighed. At the end of each day, the workers were paid in cash for the number of pounds they'd picked. Mama kept a tally of the money in a small notebook. She was the bank.

Picking cotton together was how our family averted financial disaster and saved enough money to purchase a small home back in Tucson. When we moved back, Mama went to work as a car hop waitress at Duke's Drive-in, a black-owned restaurant that had opened on Main Street near Dunbar School. She worked there until she was hired at the Young Women's Christian Association (YWCA) as a housekeeper in the residence area.

-Lucille Warner-

When I returned to Dunbar to finish the second grade, I was placed in the classroom of one of the most formidable teachers I would ever have in life. Lucille Warner was one of those teachers one can never forget. She was a very heavyset, tallish, dark-skinned woman who was not to be messed with. She was large—very large. She literally swayed when she walked, and she had a large voice. It could be warm and sweet at times, but she could also speak very sternly. Usually, her voice was enough to keep students under control. Miss Warner was an excellent teacher because she could command her students' attention. No one dared to get too far out of line with Miss Warner. When she strolled her large body over to your seat, it usually was not to pay you a warm, fuzzy visit—especially if she had a ruler in her hand! We learned to read, write, and do our arithmetic in her room; she did not negotiate alternatives to learning. "Time on task"—keeping at your work in today's educational jargon—was the silent motto in Lucille Warner's second grade classroom.

Miss Warner also doubled as the nurse when emergencies arose if our school nurse did not happen to be around. For a time, she was my daily nurse. Every single day I would get a hemorrhaging nosebleed in class—every day! I'd bleed what seemed like a bucket of blood in the girls' bathroom sink. Miss Warner would patiently stand by my side, holding my head back, wiping away the blood, and folding wet paper towels to place under my top lip inside my mouth. Eventually, the bleeding would stop and both of us would return to the classroom, well spotted with crimson stains. This went on for weeks until the nurse finally advised my mother to have my nose cauterized in a doctor's office. After the medical procedure, I never bled in school again. Both Miss Warner and I were greatly relieved.

What I liked most about Lucille Warner was that she was accountable. She believed herself to be the bottom line in our educational experience while she was in charge of it. There was no such thing as special education or gifted education in our school. There were a wide range of abilities along the bell curve, to be sure, and she had them all in her classroom to deal with. Miss Warner sought no excuses. She taught at multiple levels of cognition in order to reach us all. There were a lot of students in her class, as there were in all of the classes at Dunbar. She did not take this as cause to slack or to complain; she worked it out so that we were all taught. Peer tutoring and cooperative learning methodologies must have been invented at Dunbar, because we students often pitched in to help each other learn.

Additionally, Miss Warner required that we learn hygiene and etiquette. Every day she inspected our hands and fingernails for cleanliness. We also had to have a clean handkerchief to place over our mouths when we coughed or sneezed. Was that not the responsibility of the home? Not exclusively, according to Miss Warner's perspective. The school had a role to play in the development of pro-social skills as well as academic ones. How quaint. How rational. How wonderful. How lucky we students were!

-Josie Daniels-

When pretty Miss Daniels said, "Good morning, boys and girls," it was the first time that I had heard a real Southern accent falling from the lips of a black person. At least, it was the first time I'd noticed it. Petite, genteel, and utterly charming, Miss Daniels was to be my fourth grade teacher. I liked her right from the start. She was just as pretty as Miss Hambright, my third grade teacher, had been. Her light brown skin with light freckles sprinkled across her high cheekbones reminded me faintly of my mother. She and Mama were about the same age, but Miss Daniels was unmarried, and this was her first job. .Josie was a Texan; exactly where in Texas she was from I don't know, but my guess is Houston. Her drawl was distinctive, though she spoke grammatically impeccable English. Morgan Maxwell would have that no other way.

When a local radio station invited our school to participate in a kind of academic decathlon, a competition that pitted students from our school against students from one of the white schools, Miss Daniels chose Charles McCray and me to represent our grade. For weeks before the broadcast, she and other teachers drilled us on geography, history, and literature facts. We missed recess and often ate in the classroom at lunchtime. While the other girls in our class were drooling over the new boy—tall, dark, and handsome Eddie Mitchell—I was stuck in a room memorizing the names of lakes and rivers in Michigan! Fairness was moot; the situation was nonnegotiable

All of Tucson's students were being taught the same curriculum, theoretically—even though our textbooks were usually handed down from white schools, torn and worn out after the white school adopted brand-new ones—so the questions were to come from a pool of common knowledge. The winning contestants would take a new radio back to their home school.

On the day of the competition, I was so nervous my knees knocked underneath the table. Charles appeared more composed, and he was so smart. His mother was a wonderful schoolteacher, and it showed. With the precision of a clock's second hand, Charles could recall dates and facts that we were required to know at our grade level. He was unstoppable.

Charles's demeanor shored me up. To my surprise, I did well through the areas in which I felt weak: geography, history, and math. Then came spelling, my *strongest* area (or so I thought). I had it made, and we were winning... until I was asked to spell the word "tomorrow." Confidently, I barked out the letters: "t-o-m-m-o-r-r-o-w!"

My teammates' faces fell a mile. It took me a second to realize what I had done wrong. The word had only one *m* in it. We lost, and the other school took home the radio. I was mortified. My mother had everybody at the YWCA, where she worked, listening, not to mention that every student in Dunbar was glued to the radio. How would I ever face my teacher? *My* tomorrow would be shattered by shame!

Mama was pretty upset. "You knew how to spell that word!" she said.

So was Miss Daniels. But Mr. Maxwell seemed to take the situation well.

He actually took me out of class and teased me a little the next day. "Since when did tomorrow grow another *m*?" he asked me, pretending to be angry. Then, observing my scared, rigid demeanor, he relaxed the frown on his face, tossed his head to the side, tickled me under my chin, and uttered a loud guffaw. "We'll get 'em next time," he said, while patting me on the back reassuringly. I felt a lot better.

I was pretty certain there would be no "next time" for me. But I was wrong. To my surprise, when the next opportunity to compete in a similar contest came up, Miss Daniels selected me again. To this day, I don't understand why she would take a second chance with me (there were lots of other really smart students in our class: Minnie Faye Anderson, Irene Height, Patricia Davenport, and Arlena Brooks, to name a few) but she did. Also to this day, I'm eternally grateful.

My self-confidence had taken a hard tumble after my blunder in the first episode of competing. I was not in any hurry to risk epic failure again. But, Josie Daniels saw my potential to succeed, dismissed her disappointment in my initial performance, and gave me the second chance that saved my life…well, at least my *dignity*.

I held up my end, and the team was victorious. We won and took that radio back to Dunbar! I've never forgotten how it felt to fail and then come back to win. It was awesome. Years later, I realized that this had been her intention—precisely.

-Sidney Dawson-

If Sid Dawson ever reads this story, he will wonder why I, of all people, included him. Mr. Dawson was the award-winning choir teacher at Dunbar. I was never known for my singing voice. Eva Bazy, Gwendolyn Sparks, Thelma Andrews, Harvey Adams, Barbara Nell Mathis, and Elnora Washington, among others, were the songbirds of Dunbar. I was a member of our renowned Dunbar Chorus, but no one ever asked me to sing a solo. My "angelic" voice had not yet emerged.

But Mr. Dawson did something else for me—he allowed me to stay in his room to eat lunch every day while one of the most gifted young musicians I've ever known practiced piano. Ralston Pitts was an eighth grade wonder who had recently moved to Arizona from someplace in the Midwest to live with his foster mother and two other siblings, William and Margaret. He was very talented and loved to play classical and popular music. Mr. Dawson let him use the piano during lunch break, and I was allowed to keep him company. We became good friends, but equally important, I became exposed to really good music composed by the masters.

Ralston played Mozart and Chopin as well as one of the classic hit songs of that day, "Deep Purple." To watch Ralston become enveloped in a sonata was quite magical: he would sway rhythmically with the music as he moved nimble fingers effortlessly up and down the ivories of the keyboard. Sometimes, when he was playing something bravado, he'd literally raise his body up off the bench in sort of a bouncing motion. He was really into it whenever he did that.

Significantly, Ralston let me sing. "Sing the chorus," he'd say. Then he would cover his ears playfully (or maybe not). But about as often as not, he would praise my efforts—even when I screeched on the high notes in my favorite song, "Trees," a beautiful poem written by Joyce Kilmer and subsequently set to music by Oscar Rasbach in the early 1900s.[1] I seriously began to think I had a good voice. Much like many of the less-than-talented *American Idol* hopefuls, I still do. Denial, as they say, is not just a river in Africa.

-William Hudson-

Like Mr. Dawson, Mr. Hudson, who was a history teacher, would be shocked that he was so significant in my formative life. He never taught me a single history lesson. I barely knew him at all, except in one capacity—he headed the annual school fundraiser the year I sold the most carnival raffle tickets. I won the title of "Queen," along with a clear vinyl hairbrush and comb set as my prize. Though I didn't know it then, I was on my way to a sales and marketing career with the McGraw-Hill Companies, many years later, which would expand my world and my financial fortune exponentially. It is the world from which I am now retired.

It was a long, long distance from that contest at Dunbar to a national sales office in Monterey, California, working in sales and marketing for a huge, international publishing company headquartered in New York. But I learned something at Dunbar about my ability to work long hours and talk persuasively to prospective customers that would serve me very well down the road of life. What if Mr. Hudson had not set a sales goal for me and encouraged me to

---

1   http://www.cs.rice.edu/~ssiyer/minstrels/poems/146.html

keep going until I reached it? Why, that was how I came to make my living. Who would've thunk it?

In the process, I learned why sales is called the numbers game. You see, I lived farther from Dunbar than almost anyone else, except the kids from "A" Mountain, the mountain located on the far west side of town where a giant letter *A*, for Arizona, was whitewashed on its side to identify it and the home of the University of Arizona. They and the South Park kids had to ride a bus to and from school. But I would walk the entire "sales territory" from Dunbar to my house (about seven miles), selling tickets at every home and business establishment along the way. Since we lived in the direction of the U of A and near the eastern suburbs, this strategy exposed me to a select set of buyers, mostly whites, who had both the means and the inclination to purchase a few ten-cent tickets from "such a sweet and charming young black girl."

Playful vanity aside, I really did have a set of pearly white teeth and a pretty, dimpled smile, and I knew how to use my assets to persuade. In the end, I had the numbers in my favor. Winning by outselling the competition became an unspoken aspiration to be fulfilled in a distant future when millions, not hundreds, of dollars would be the measure of success.

So who was Bill Hudson? He was actually my first marketing and sales manager. But, he was not my last. Ben Hicks, regional vice president of CTB/McGraw-Hill's southern division, under whose leadership I worked for seven years as evaluation marketing and sales consultant, gets that distinction. Outside the door of Mr. Hudson's classroom in the hall, there was a bronze bust of George Washington Carver, former slave, scientist, and teacher. To this day, I can still see his facial features and the words of wisdom that were imprinted on the small plaque attached to the bust. I committed them to memory. They are words that have guided my life ever since: "Start where you are with what you've got. Make something of it. Never be satisfied." That's still my life's credo.

-Kathryn Maxwell-

I had never been inside the home of a middle-class Negro until the principal's beautiful (and I mean, *beautiful*) daughter, Kathryn

Maxwell, (she was named after her mother) cut her finger and chose me to help her out with a chore at home. She was a brand-new teacher, or perhaps she was just a substitute teacher (I'm not sure which) at our school. She asked me one day to go to the home where she lived with her parents and wash the dishes. This would never happen today, but it was not something we even blinked about in that day. The house was only two or three blocks from the school. She gave me the key and paid me fifty cents to take care of the dirty dishes, which I assumed was her assigned chore, since she still lived at home. I left school after lunch and went down the street to the Maxwell house.

After entering, I walked through the home in sheer wonderment, taking in the entire ambiance. There were French provincial furniture pieces; a real, log-burning fireplace; hardwood floors; and ceramic-tiled kitchen counters. *And* there were framed photographs on the mantel and lamp tables—pictures of a husband and wife close together, smiling (as if they were in love), pictures of their son and daughter as children, photos that captured babyhood and early childhood and teenage through college years.

By contrast, there were no such pictures in my house. To my knowledge, there is only one baby picture of me (at about two years old), and there are no pictures of my brother until we were seven and eight years old.

I include this story because the experience represents a pivotal episode in the shaping of my aspirations. It was the first time I saw someone I knew, who was also black, living well, and truly happy. My perception of what was possible changed that day.

-Minnie Earl Marshall-

Near the end of my sixth grade year at Dunbar, I began encountering a very attractive young black woman who walked in the opposite direction from mine as I was on my way to school walking from Mama's job at the Y. She was tall, very slender, and shaped like no one I'd ever seen, except in magazines. She walked swan-like, taking each step with grace and poise. Feet pointed outward, she seemed to place each step deliberately. Her way of walking was truly poetry in motion to a gangly, awkward preteen like me. Always, always, she smiled broadly and waved to me from across the street. I didn't know who she was or where she was going, but I liked her so much. I began imitating her walk, as best as I could, after we passed each other. That was a funny sight, I'm sure. Actually, I don't think anyone could imitate her successfully; she was in a class alone.

The following fall, Minnie Earl Marshall introduced herself to me and my other seventh grade classmates who stood before her nervously tugging at our ill-fitting blue-bloomered gym suits in the gymnasium of Dunbar School. She was to be our new PE teacher. Aha! Now I understood. Minnie Earl was on her way to the University of Arizona when I would pass her walking so beautifully. I later learned that she was one of the star dancers in the modern dance troupe that the university was so proud of. What's more, she had been privileged to study in Harlem, New York, with the famous dancer, Martha Graham. No greater talent had ever come from among us. She was an icon of poised and graceful femininity. And, she was black, like me. Minnie Earl had come to teach tennis, but she taught me much, much more.

-Laura Nobles Banks-

Some people just have an air about them that makes them appear above reproach. Laura Nobles was one of those people. Always immaculately dressed and coiffed, she set an example of being "together" that we young women-to-be had to take note of. Make-up, hair, nails, nylons, heels, dresses—all perfectly coordinated, all the time. And Miss Nobles always smelled so pretty. Her pace was quick; she walked fast, spoke at a business-like clip, and moved about the classroom very purposefully. Miss Nobles was no slacker. Imitating her was not easy, although plenty of us girls tried—especially the part about stuffing our brassieres with toilet paper to try to look like Laura did in the chest area of her shapely frame. Her endowment was enviable, to say the least. I don't know any pubescent lassie who actually succeeded in pulling it off. We must have looked utterly ridiculous.

Miss Nobles's most memorable contribution to me was the time she knocked on the door at my house and asked to come in to talk with my parents. I thought I was in serious trouble! But, no, Miss Nobles just wanted to see where my brother and I lived, and to see if we had a place to study and do homework. She sat and met with my mother face to face in her own space. This struck me as being how parent-teacher conferences ought to take place. One look spoke volumes to a trained educator's eye. Understandings like this cannot be achieved in the formality of a school office or classroom. After that, Mama became more interested in what I had to say about my schoolwork and she took more time observing what I showed her. Laura Nobles, who was also the leader of my Girl Scout troop, would show up at Southside Baptist Church during Scout Week. I would give a little speech. Miss Nobles was always there to hear it, seated among the congregation and smiling her approval.

Most people will remember the high-stepping Miss Laura Nobles (who became Mrs. Banks after marrying the town's most successful black entrepreneur, Jack Banks, owner of the barbecue restaurant where we hung out and ate out) as the Laura Nobles who led our drum majorettes to one championship after another during Rodeo Week. It was our favorite time of the year. We got to show up and show out. No one could beat us! I often wonder where all of those trophies went after Dunbar was closed. Many will remember those things about Mrs. Laura Banks, but I will also remember that Mrs. Laura Nobles Banks was my fifth grade teacher.

Before leaving Dunbar, I was fortunate to have been taught by Irene Mahone, Etta Jackson, Daisy Lipscomb, Effie Edwards, and Charles Todd. So many faces, so many memories, too few pages to tell it all...

The Village

-The Hendersons-

The only family that I remember from my preschool years was somewhat in the category of the Maxwells, in terms of economics, but not quite as elegantly. They were the Hendersons. When we first moved to Tucson from Safford, we lived for a time in the rental house they owned that was situated on the back lot of their property. I was about three or four years old. They were also "middle class" and had a nice home. Mrs. Henderson would let me in whenever I wandered up to their back door. I loved to smell the scent of the Lifebuoy bath soap wafting out from the small bathroom that was just inside the door on the back porch. They actually had two bathrooms. The other one was larger and had a tile shower. These were things (tile and showers) I'd never seen before. The Hendersons talked "proper." They were from the East Coast. Like the Maxwells, they, too, had a beautiful daughter; Alice seemed like a princess to me. She was kind and gentle when I was around, and she let me play with her beautiful dolls. She was very special to her parents. They treated her like I wanted to be treated, always hugging her and smiling at her.

Alice's aunt, Ms. Cornelius, was also a very proper lady. She was well-educated—you could tell by the big words she always used when she talked. Every time she saw me, she talked about how I would grow up to be a fine young lady, get a good education, and become an AKA. She belonged to the Alpha Kappa Alpha Greek sorority. Her membership was a great source of pride to her. She talked about cultural things like plays and books and encouraged me to take interest in them as I grew up. Ms. Cornelius attended national conventions in other states and let me look through the programs when she came over to share her experiences with her sister and brother-in-law and her niece, Alice. She said I should go to a school called Howard University when I grew up. I later learned that the prestigious black school was located in Washington DC. It seemed like a very long way from Tucson. I doubted that I'd ever go there.

-Reverend Dabner-

Mr. Hill belonged to the storefront Baptist church pastored by his uncle, the Reverend Samuel Alfred Dabner. He revered his uncle, whom he called "Uncle Sam." After he and Mama were married, she joined the church too, and we all attended every Sunday. In fact, we attended almost every day. At least it seemed so to me. There was Sunday school, teacher's meeting on Tuesday nights, prayer meeting on Wednesday nights, missionary meetings on Thursday night, and we had to clean up the church every Saturday.

Eventually, Reverend Dabner built a real church. Then we had to go to church early enough to dust the burgundy-colored vinyl pew cushions on Sunday mornings and prepare the church for services. At night, we were the last to leave. We pulled the seats up and covered things that shouldn't get dusty before turning out the lights. Junior and I especially liked "First Sundays" (the first Sunday in each month was Communion Sunday). It was the day we could drink all the leftover grape juice from the communion glasses before we washed them. We were at church all day many a Sunday. There was Sunday school, eleven o'clock service, singing conventions, and BYPU (Baptist Young People's Union) in the evening before night worship service for everyone else.

Reverend Dabner was an illustrious sort of guy. He was kind of flashy in his own peculiar way. For instance, he bought a new car every year, usually a Pontiac sedan. He also chomped on fat, smelly cigars and wore nice three-piece suits. A gold pocket watch attached to a long chain was always tucked into his vest. He took it out and checked the time frequently. He was a short, slight-built man, but his persona was large. He talked a lot about money, and usually had a good-sized wad of bills in his pocket. One way he "wooed" us kids into coming to Sunday school was to give us a couple of nickels to put into the offering plate and one to buy a Popsicle after church. He would also pick us up from our homes in his fine automobile and carry us to church. This was a real treat for a bunch of poor kids along his route. Some of my first friends were among the scraggily crew that constituted this group of Sunday-schoolers; a couple of them still are my friends: Vonceil Weaver and her sister, Opal, for example.

At one point, Rev. Dabner leased a large, gray, stuccoed building near downtown Tucson that had been vacated by a failed bakery. He turned it into a rooming house. The address was three sixty South Convent. There were three wide steps attached to the sidewalk that led right up to the two front doors that were angled to coordinate with the street corner because the building formed a right angle with two intersecting streets.

Tommy and Greeta Scott lived down the street. Bobby and Harvey Adams lived directly across, and Ruby and Eddie Gentry were neighbors to the south. My family moved into the boarding house and lived there for about a year.

While living in the boarding house on Convent Street, I remember sleeping outside all night once because "the world was coming to an end" and I didn't want to miss it. I was six years old going on seven when three Jehovah's Witnesses came to the front door of the rooming house. They knocked persistently until Mama answered the door. A tall white man carrying his suit coat over his arm and wearing a tie and a white shirt with the sleeves rolled up was standing on the top step. The others, a short, black woman and a stoic-looking white woman accompanied him. While he spoke in rapid-fire sentences, they nodded their heads in agreement and clutched bibles and colorful pamphlets in their hands. Curious about the noise, I followed close behind my mother listening to the adults talk while pretending to tie my shoes.

"We stopped by to tell you that Jehovah is coming for his angels tonight, and you and your family need to be saved so you can go back to heaven with him together," the large balding white man said, wiping sweat from his round, red face. I was terrified by his words. Visions of thunder and lightning and a gigantic bearded white man dressed in white robes descending slowly from the sky filled my head. What they described was a terrible, tumultuous event that was to

take place within hours that very day! It would be something so cataclysmic, so catastrophic that humans would not be able to compre-
hend…and on and on.

Mama thanked them, calmly took the pamphlets, closed the
door, and laid the papers on the mail table in the foyer. She didn't
speak a word about what she (and I) had just heard. She just proceeded with whatever she had been doing before the interruption and
admonished me to do the same. All day, I felt tense and nervous. The
ominous warning about the coming of a large and powerful-looking
white man was all I could think of. What would happen to me? What
would happen to my dolls? My family? Would this Jehovah person
take me to live in a place called heaven? Was I "saved" enough? Would
he claim *me*? I wasn't at all sure I wanted to go; but, if this was to be
my inevitable fate, I certainly wanted to be awake when it happened;
of this I was very sure.

I begged Mama to let me sleep on the old cot that was stationed
against the back wall of the house. It was hot; I only needed a sheet to
cover the flimsy, water-stained mattress. Finally, she agreed.

Needless to say, my all-night vigil was fruitless. The world
remained intact, and the big, robed Jehovah remained in the elusive
place called heaven. My consummate relief was mixed with disappointment; fantasy was betrayed by reality. By dawn, everything went
back to being the same. That was in the year 1945. Since then, I have
heard no less than a hundred such warnings of doom and pending
end-time apocalypse prognosticated by a variety of religious prophets.
None of them have come true.

Reverend Dabner had a room in the building also. I could often
hear him humming church tunes and practicing his preaching. I
always knew what the Sunday sermon would sound like.

There was a fervor about him that was infectious. In the pulpit,
his preaching style emulated so many other Baptist preachers I've
heard since those days: he would start out speaking slowly as he led
up to his text for the day. In the beginning, he would toss in a bit of
humor just to warm the congregation up. As he got into his sermon,
he seemed to wind up. Where he once spoke in a clear, modulated
voice, he would change and begin to speak in a sort of sing-song,
whiney voice. At pitch, he would commence to cry and spew spittle

in every direction. As he ran back and forth across the pulpit, tears streaming down his face, he held a white handkerchief up to his ears, as if his high-pitched shouting hurt them. In the course of a single sermon, he could use up to six or seven clean handkerchiefs, which he kept stacked under the podium. His face would be dripping sweat and tears by the time he was finished, and he needed an overcoat to cover his sweat-soaked suit. This kept him from catching a cold, I suppose. I still see this practiced in black Baptist churches today.

I truly believed that Reverend Dabner was a man of God, though some of his behavior left questions in my mind. I couldn't get it, for example, when, at age fifty, he dumped Miss Clara Ward, the gregarious, buxom, middle-aged woman he had been romantically associated with for years, to marry a wispy young woman half his age. Eyebrows were raised way high. Some members left the church because of this; most stayed. The couple survived the storm and remained married for the next forty-five or so years until Reverend Dabner's death. They appeared to live happily as well.

What I remember most is that, as one of my most significant community teachers, Reverend Dabner sold me on the concept of God as savior. I became a Christian and was baptized in the small baptismal pool situated behind the pulpit of his beloved church, Southside Baptist. I was twelve years old. I'm still learning, at sixty-nine, what it means to live like a Christian.

-Mrs. Buggs-

I don't know why my mind runs to Mrs. Buggs right at this moment. I hardly knew her at all. She was a small-framed, white-haired, part white, part Negro woman who lived near our home on Campbell Ave. To my knowledge, she had no children or grandchildren of her own; she was either a spinster or a widow. She lived alone in a very nice house. Periodically she must have felt pretty lonely, because she would invite all of us black kids in the neighborhood (all seven of us) to play croquet in her spacious, green backyard, which was enclosed in a high brick wall. Although I never went inside, Mrs. Buggs entertained us graciously by serving cookies, homemade lemonade, and sometimes ice cream from her back porch. It was a magnanimous display of kindness that left a big imprint on my young psyche. To a poor kid like me, it was a wonderful demonstration of unsolicited human kindness. I appreciate her to this very day.

-Irving Pierce-

Irving Pierce was another of those people who I barely knew. In fact, I only knew him as an acquaintance who befriended my close friend, Lola Andrews, and her six brothers and sisters: Vernon, Clarence, Ira, Thelma, Katy, and Hallene, who were being reared by a single parent, their father. Every Sunday, Mr. Pierce as we called him, would cook an enormous meal. All of the Andrews kids were invited over for dinner after church; I tagged along. My objective was to spend the afternoons visiting my girlfriend, instead of going home (across town) and returning to attend BYPU and evening services. But, I couldn't help looking forward to smothered pork chops, rice and gravy, collard greens, sweet potatoes, potato salad, corn bread, and peach cobbler. There was always just such a spread.

I really don't know why Mr. Pierce was motivated to buy and cook so much food every week. He fed whoever showed up, laughing and joking with us all the way. His joy seemed to derive from seeing us scarf down the food until we were stuffed. Teenagers could eat a lot. Mrs. Pierce quietly assisted him, but he was the one who "got high" on those fun-filled Sundays. For me, having a warm, friendly, safe place to go was a godsend. It was a temporary escape from a troubled home life that often left me feeling helpless and vulnerable. Whatever his motivation, I owe a debt of gratitude to Mr. Pierce. His generosity of time, resources, and spirit remains among my fondest memories of caring people.

Friends

-Daisy Lewis-

I really only had one constant neighborhood playmate growing up. This was Daisy Lewis. I sometimes played with Virginia Basurto, who lived next door with her grandparents, and now and then I played with Patsy Baskerville whenever she visited her godparents, Tommy and Hazel Williams. These girls were both younger than I was and not nearly as interesting to me at the time as was Daisy. She lived around the corner with her grandmother, Mrs. Dorchester. I lived on Campbell Avenue; they lived on Thirteenth Street. The Dorchester's backyard wire fence, however, ran along the alley that was often used as a shortcut from my backyard to the Safeway market on North Broadway. It was a great meeting place for us friends. Lingering there too long got me into *mucho* trouble more than once! I just couldn't break the habit.

Daisy and I would play paper dolls together. Whenever one of us got a new punch-out book of dolls and clothing, we'd run over to check them out. Well, usually I'd run over to Daisy's house. We didn't have much room in our house for spreading out playthings. It was always fun. She was very imaginative.

The thing I like most to remember about my friendship with Daisy is that I was allowed to go downtown with her to buy things when we were both old enough to ride the public bus. Before we returned home, Daisy always had to pick out a gift for her grandmother. It was a rule in their household that she remember to bring some little trinket back for her grandparent. She did that for as long as I knew her. I wish now that I had taught my kids to be thoughtful in that way.

Once, when I got into a fight after school (my one and only), a big crowd gathered to watch Jannie Chapple beat me up. Daisy came over and stood at the edge of the crowd. It was the first (and last) time I ever played "the dozens"—word rhymes that usually involved insulting someone's mama. Soon, the verbal part of the fight took on the characteristics of a drunken sailors' brawl; the language became very crude. I'd had virtually no experience arguing in this manner, so I was losing. I was pretty scared. My friend, Daisy, on the other hand, was not easily intimidated. When I was looking quite pitiful in her view, she (and others in the crowd) began to shout out things I could say back to Jannie. They were not very nice rhymes (the dozens typically are not nice), but I said them anyway. I wanted to win this battle of words.

Jannie was stunned! She never imagined that I could utter such vitriolic garbage. So was everyone else. I still hang my head in shame when I think about that event. The fight was broken up by the school's safety patrol captain. He led both of us to the office. Mr. Maxwell looked shocked to see *me* in trouble. Jannie was no stranger; she was in there regularly for one infraction or another, but never *me*! I began to cry from embarrassment, but that didn't save me from the punishment: three swats with a paddle. Rules were rules. What was worse was that I was late for my ride home with my mother, who had been waiting for me at the Y. When I looked up and saw her enter the office, I knew I was in *real* trouble. The ride home was the longest one I can ever remember. Another spanking awaited me, of which I was certain. I was not disappointed; it was a vigorous one—first for what happened at school, and second for being late. It was a hurtful day all around! I never fought, nor played the dozens again.

The two of us could find other ways to get into trouble with our parents. My stepfather spanked me more than once for "dawdling" at Daisy's back fence to gossip while he was waiting for bread, flour, or some other necessity from my errand to the grocery store, with which to finish a meal. Blah, blah, blah, blah. We just couldn't stop talking.

Then there was the time we begged her grandmother to let her go to my job with me. It was a short-term summer job; I was helping out my swimming instructor from the Y, Mrs. Jones. I was only eleven years old, but I knew how to clean a house and prepare vegetables for cooking: washing and peeling potatoes, carrots, onions, and celery. I was paid five dollars to go out to her house near the foothills on the bus after summer day camp and put things in order. She had broken her arm and needed a little assistance at home. I was grateful to be able to earn the money to buy new school clothes.

The day Daisy went with me, we did everything except what I was hired to do. We made sandwiches and lemonade and set ourselves up in the living room to eat in front of the large, plate glass window. When the bus went by, people could see us, and we thought they would believe we lived there. We got a lot of pleasure out of thinking up that little hoax. But, the fun evaporated when Mrs. Jones's car drove up a half-hour early, and we hadn't done a stitch of work.

Once again, my mother was summoned, and there was a good-sized penance to pay for that escapade. I was grounded from visiting Daisy for a good spell, and I was not allowed to take Mrs. Jones's money, even though I still had to do the work. Fortunately, I wasn't fired, but Daisy never accompanied me to work again. I was lucky to keep my little job—lucky it was Mrs. Jones I was working for.

Because of where her house was located in the neighborhood and the fact that her grandmother did not work outside the home, Daisy never experienced the sexual harassment of a neighbor who was a predator. He was a retired army officer who lived across the street from our house. Because I love his ex-wife and their children, I will leave him nameless in this story. The large, muscular black man would touch, pinch, and bite my thighs. I was never sexually assaulted to the point of rape, but I was petrified to leave the screen door unlatched whenever I was home alone on Saturdays or during the summer. He would walk right in and begin chasing me through the house. I was terrified whenever I saw him crossing the street heading in the direction of our house. I never told Daisy about this. I never told anyone, until now.

Daisy and I had a mutual teenage friend, Edith Butler, who was the third black girl in our neighborhood; she lived on Thirteenth Street too. Edith (nicknamed Cookie) did not attend public school. She and her brothers, Kenneth and Sonny, went to Catholic school. From time to time, we visited each other's homes, but she was beyond playing paper dolls; her interests were more advanced than ours; she was into popular music, boys, and dates. I was still wetting the bed.

-Rosetta-

Although Daisy and Edith were certainly my good friends and neighbors, my very best friend since first grade and to this day has been Rosetta Williams. She did not go to Miss Shaw's nursery school, so we met when we were almost six years old in Mrs. Carter's first grade class (there was no kindergarten). We could only play together at school because we lived miles apart. Rosetta was very smart, especially in mathematics. As we grew older, she recognized how I struggled with arithmetic and often let me copy answers to homework from her papers. We would sit next to each other as often as teachers would allow it (we also talked a lot in class and were sometimes separated to keep us quiet). In school, we balanced each other's strengths and helped each other. Though our homes were not close, we used the telephone (for a short time) to connect after school and carry on our unending conversations. I left Rosetta at John Springs, the renamed Dunbar school when I was transferred to Mansfeld Junior High, but we always remained friends.

The Big Transition

I was finishing the seventh grade in the spring of 1951 when the Tucson Board of Trustees decided to end de facto segregation of its schools. Dunbar School would be no more according to the new school board ruling. The name would be changed from Paul Laurence Dunbar, the namesake of a highly revered black poet and educator, to John Springs Junior High School, in honor of a white pioneer and settler. Tears and pleas were ignored by the board and the district's superintendent, Robert Morrow. We had just gotten used to the shiny new annex that had provided additional classrooms, a new gymnasium, cafeteria, and water fountains that worked. Now we would be separated and disbursed to unfamiliar schools, teachers, and classmates, according to where we lived in the city. This was to be the solution to de facto segregation, but it felt to me more like the legendary *diaspora* that our slave ancestors experienced so long ago. It was an unwelcome change. Fear of separation and isolation consumed my thoughts.

The news dealt a devastating blow to the morale of students and faculty alike. Morally, we knew it was the right thing to do, but it felt like surgery without anesthesia to most of us. There were many adjustments to be made ahead.

For the hefty sum of two thousand dollars, my mother negotiated a real estate deal for a three-room house on South Campbell Avenue, between East Broadway and Thirteenth Street. By the time we reached junior high age, Daisy had moved back to Chicago where her family was from. Except for Johnny Sanders, who lived on Thirteenth Street, the only other black kids old enough to go to junior high (Kenneth, Edith, and Harry "Sonny" Butler) attended Catholic school. James Hollins was still too young, though he also lived on Campbell Ave. That meant I would enroll in Mansfeld Junior High

School as the first and only black female student. It was preparation for many future experiences wherein I would be the first black person in an organization, and often the "token" one. This was to be de facto desegregation, and I was assigned to attend the nearest school to my residence. It was the "neighborhood school" concept, of which I, as a mature educator, today, am very fond. But back then, I was very anxious and more than a little scared of what I was about to confront. It was fear of the unknown, and it was real.

-Mansfeld Days, Mansfeld Ways-

Mansfeld Junior High was a large school with a reputation for being academically challenging. The students were largely from socially and economically affluent homes (though some definitely were not). Doctors, lawyers, and merchants kids went to Mansfeld. The social as well as the academic pace was pretty swift. If it had not been for the first two girls who befriended me, Irma Flores and Mary*,[1] I don't know how I would have survived the loneliness I felt that first semester. I missed my Dunbar classmates and the teachers I had known since first grade. I no longer felt safe, secure, intellectually capable, and accepted. Mostly, initially, I felt displaced, dumb, and discouraged.

Some people did not believe the integration ruling was right; among those who disagreed were some of the teachers at Mansfeld. Those teachers had trouble masking their displeasure that I was now a student in the formerly all-white school. Although the students adjusted to the idea fairly quickly, a couple of my teachers told me that I was not prepared to handle the rigor of their curriculum, but that was just too bad; it was my problem, not theirs. In my heart, I knew they were wrong; I had been a good student at Dunbar. I was used to As and Bs. Nevertheless, I floundered on some occasions when I felt hemmed in and unsure of myself. One such occasion was when my history teacher went around the room asking students to

---

1   I have changed all names followed by an asterisk in this book. The reasons vary: some are friends whom I don't wish to hurt by this writing, and at least one is a person I knew in a professional capacity and have chosen to disguise the name.

tell what part of the world their ancestors were from. I remember dreading that it would soon be my turn and I would have to say Africa. In those days, Africa was considered the "Dark Continent," a place where savages went around naked and cannibalized each other (that's what the media portrayed). It was not a place to be proud to call one's ancestral home. Even among blacks, to be called an African was an insult that could ignite enough of a spark to start a fist fight. I knew how this teacher stood on the question of school integration, and didn't want to give her the satisfaction of hearing my classmates snicker (I thought they would) when I gave my answer. When she called on me, I answered boldly, "Belgium." Frankly, I didn't have a clue where Belgium was, but it sounded better than Africa just then.

"You mean, the Belgian Congo, don't you?" she asked in a syrupy sweet voice.

"No Ma'am," I answered defiantly, "I'm from Belgium."

I was determined not to be embarrassed, even if it meant telling a whopping lie.

She looked at me askance, but, mercifully, moved on without further probing.

When I got my first report card, it contained Cs and Ds for the first time in my life. I was in trouble. Students at this new school were academically competitive—very competitive! They argued vigorously in civics and history classes, compared grades on each and every test, and lobbied teachers for higher scores, often succeeding. They verbally kibitzed with one another all the time on one topic or another. The work was hard, and there was always a lot of it. It was a stimulating environment, to say the least.

-Gracie Hirleman-

Although the principal, Mr. Anderson, the choir teacher, Mr. Sayers, and Coach Jones were among some of the teaching staff who tried to make me feel welcome, one teacher at that school stands out in my memory as my highest personal advocate: Miss Gracie Hirleman. Like Miss Warner, Miss Hirleman was a no-nonsense person. She must have been about sixty-five years old (which seemed old when I was thirteen). Her hair was soft, pure white, parted in the middle, braided, and pinned at the nape of her neck. As the day wore on, she perspired, and wisps of white hair crept out of the neat coif and fell freely around her fair-complexioned face. She was medium-built, and the dresses she wore were usually of the homemade variety. They were gingham floral prints that stopped well below her calves and swished when she walked, stiffened by the light starch that she ironed into the soft, cotton fabric. When Miss Hirleman spoke, it wasn't in a loud voice, but everyone shut up and listened to her words. Like Miss Warner, she was not to be messed with. She was all business.

Miss Hirleman was my English teacher. She made me rewrite many an essay because it was either illegible (by her handwriting standards) or just not what she thought was my best work. At first, I resented her for being so critical. I was sure she was picking on me because I was black. I didn't like feeling inferior, but that's just how I felt.

Then one day she kept me after class for a little talk. She took my face into her thin, wrinkled right hand, put the other one on her hip (her favorite stance), and pulled me as close as possible to her. She pursed those tiny, pink lips of hers and read me the riot act! She told me she knew I was trying to adjust to a lot of new things but that she was not there to feel sorry for me—she was there to teach me every-thing I would need to know to do well at the next level of school. "Besides," she said, "You don't need anybody's sympathy! You're as capable as anybody in this class and more capable than most. So, take that chip off your shoulder and get to work doing your best. I expect top-notch work out of you, young lady, and that's what you're going to give me!"

It was a stinging reprimand. I shall never forget it; nor shall I ever forget Gracie Hirleman, who, at the end of my ninth-grade year, took great pride in personally presenting me with the award for Highest Honors before an audience of the entire student body. I had made straight As in every subject for the entire year. I love Miss Hirleman to this day for confronting me about myself. She was not indiffer-ent, nor was she rude. She just wanted me to understand that I was responsible for myself—my attitudes and my performance. It was as simple as that. With her help, I was on my way to a big turning point.

According to all of the literature that I read today concerning underachievement of black students in public schools, the major cause is not lack of ability but the failure of students to connect the dots between *effort* and learning, which, when applied, more often than not, results in high academic achievement. Miss Hirleman helped me to make that connection at a critical time in my life. Just when I was ready to give up out of self-doubt, she intervened. She didn't let me off the hook with sympathy or by giving me less rigorous work than I was capable of handling. By accurately assessing my capacity to perform and requiring that I push myself harder, she helped me reach the higher bars of achievement. I overcame my insecurities there in that place called Mansfeld and regained a lost sense of self-efficacy, faith in my innate abilities, and confidence that would propel me forward with positive thrust to a brighter future.

Given the situation in which I found myself, I had to decide to either get busy failing or get busy succeeding. Ultimately, I chose the latter. I was forced to cast aside my timid insecurities, my hostility over losing my Dunbar, and, to a large extent, my fierce cleavage to the stigma that black was synonymous with inferiority so I could get into the game—into the competition. This was going to be tough. I really needed a friend or two to help me get through the adjustment period.

-Irma Flores and Mary-

Irma Flores was an "integrated" kid, like me. She had attended a segregated school assigned to Hispanic students, Safford Junior High Mexicans were just as victimized by Jim Crow practices as were blacks; neither they nor we could sit downstairs in the town's movie theatres (our seats were located only in the balcony); we couldn't eat at the counter of the local five-and-dime store; and before desegregation, those of us who had lived far away from the one public school designated to serve our kind were packed into the one school bus that was assigned to our school as it circulated around the city to pick everyone up, regardless of how many students needed a ride.

We called our bus "the sardine can." It was packed to capacity by the time it reached the school; not even standing room was left. And, it stank! Every day, someone "lost their manners" en route to school. Invariably, the stale air smelled of rotten eggs; cold winter days, when windows had to be closed, were the worst. For some of the adolescent boys, passing gas was sport. Boys like that are called "gross" by girls today, and they were gross back then too.

Irma's father owned a pharmacy in town. It was a nice drugstore at the corner of Meyers Street and Congress Avenue. They lived in a spacious, red brick house nearer to the school than mine. When I transferred to Mansfeld, we walked home together every day, along with Mary, a lawyer's daughter, who liked us and walked a long part of the distance with us before turning off. After leaving Irma at her house, I still had a good distance to go to get home. We shared a lot of laughter and gossip while we walked. It was a fun stroll, which we enjoyed until Mary's father forbade her to continue walking with Irma and me. She wept as she told us how he had driven by one day, seen her walking with us, and scolded her. It was a dash of cold reality. Irma remained my friend until we graduated two years later. For that matter, so did Mary; we just had to be careful where we were seen together. Neither of us wanted to cause her to get in trouble at home. It was an awkward situation, to say the least. By then, I had earned the respect and friendship of many other classmates. I suppose one could classify that as balance.

In fact, I had had the distinction of being elected student council secretary by a plurality of students' votes in the first semester I was in attendance. I beat Alice Patterson, the girl I honestly thought was the more-qualified candidate, by a landslide. This was my first solid lesson in the concept of "qualification for the job." Although I had been council representative for the sixth grade class at Dunbar, I had never held any other office, and I did not know one thing about writing minutes. Alice, on the other hand, was a ninth grade student who had already served in Mansfeld's student council for two years. She was more familiar with what the secretary's job was, and she was much more mature than I was. I gave a moving campaign speech (according to Johnny Sanders's recollection) that won over the voters, but it was she, not I, who deserved to win.

Now that I am, once again, the recording secretary of an organization (The Fredrick Douglass Social and Charitable Women's Club of Austin), I realize the importance of good listening skills. These are the central skills that are needed for good writing of minutes. Mine were poorly developed at that juncture of my life. As a result, I struggled mightily in my new office.

I often felt that I was ostracized from the social events that took place on campus during the school day, though I'm sure the other students did not intend to make me feel this way. Once a month, for example, a "social hour" was held in the school auditorium. Its purpose was to initiate the process of socialization between genders by encouraging girls and boys to intermix conversationally and through social dancing. I despised these mandatory events. Although they would laugh and joke with me, I was never asked to dance by a single boy—not even my so-called buddies. In fact, out of sympathy for me, the tall, gray-haired, fiftyish Coach Jones would take me out on the floor and dance with me. How embarrassing! It wasn't that he was not a good dancer, he was just old. I felt like I was dancing with someone's father! After a while, I offered to spin the records. I preferred being a disc jockey. That job kept me constructively busy and allowed me to save face, but *watching* others have fun was not my idea of fun.

No one knew what a good dancer I really was until the night of the ninth grade prom. I asked Harvey Adams, a high school senior, to accompany me to the dance. Harvey was a wonderful dancer. He was smooth and graceful at waltzing and doing the jitter-bug. We took over the dance floor with our wide swings, elegant turns, and deep dips. The female teachers very nearly ruined my evening by trying to monopolize my date for dances. They were awed by Harvey's skill and charm. It was a great night.

By the time I graduated from the ninth grade, I had a plethora of new friends and acquaintances. Oddly, however, if memory serves me correctly, I was never invited into the home of a single white classmate in the two years I attended Mansfeld. Only Irma, my Mexican friend, asked me inside from time to time. Needless to say,

I didn't invite my classmates to my home, either. Our reasons were different...I think.

-Reflections-

I've pondered many times what the difference was between Mansfeld and Dunbar. I think it was this: these middle and upper class white kids from Mansfeld had lived different lives from any of us Dunbar students, including, as well, those of our all-black teachers. Never having had to deal with the stigma of Jim Crow repression, everyone in this new environment was truly *free*. They were used to speaking their minds anywhere, anytime, without fear; we Negro students, by contrast, were taught both at home and at school to hold our tongues lest our remarks be considered rude, inappropriate, or disrespectful (especially to white folks). In the social structure that we black children grew up in, overt assertiveness, rude or rebellious behavior, and an unbridled tongue could cost us dearly. The price could range from incarceration to death by an officer's bullet. These were well-known penalties for youthful bravado exercised in the wrong places at the wrong times. Compliance with adult rules was deemed preemptive protection from a harsh, cruel justice system. We were not allowed to run amok—anywhere. Dunbar students were often told to "sit down" and to "shut up!" We feared physical reprisal for "talking back" to a teacher or any other adult. We paid in spades for verbiage that called into question our levels of courtesy and respect both at home and away. Backhand slaps by our parents or other family members were not considered child abuse; nor was a whipping with a leather belt. Teachers and the principal could spank us with thick wooden paddles if we got out of line. One could say with some accuracy that we were socially repressed, whereas the white kids at Mansfeld were encouraged to express themselves with impunity. It took me a while to connect to this.

Unlike my family and the families of most of the economically deprived students I knew at Dunbar, Mansfeld students were trained both at school and at home to routinely analyze and interpret information. They questioned and demanded proof of the veracity of verbally expressed opinions as well as those that appeared in the popular press: newspapers, magazines, pamphlets, and newsletters. At home, they discussed and debated social and political issues with their parents and family friends. These were "adult" activities in our community—barber shop and beauty shop topics in which young people seldom engaged.

Although there were, to be sure, variations, in terms of relative family affluence and what that might afford among Mansfeld students, things like annual family vacations taken far away from Tucson were more the norm than not for Mansfeld kids. Extended families typically lived in Eastern, Midwestern, and West Coast states. Visits to these places provided educational bonuses that were very different from those experienced by most of Dunbar students, whose extended families were most likely to live in the rural South in states like Texas, Louisiana, Arkansas, and Mississippi where such visits only evoked further experiences of Jim Crow repression.

To the benefit of Mansfeld's white students, travel and family visits fed and nurtured the development of personal confidence and provided a body of commonly shared knowledge and understandings that supported the teaching and learning process at school. One might summarize the difference this way: whereas we—the Dunbar students (and I suspect, the other formerly segregated students, for example, the Hispanics)—intentionally or not, were taught to *focus* more on our behavior, demeanor, appearance, and attitudes, they—the white, middle- and upper-class students—were taught to *scan*, in search of new ideas, concepts, and social and economic opportunities to be exploited. In my opinion, it was the "worker versus owner" indoctrination that best characterized the difference. This analysis is not intended to demean, criticize, nor in any way marginalize the good, basic education that we received at Dunbar, but to acknowledge fundamental differences in the premises upon which the two approaches were based. While we were relentlessly taught that our futures were limitless by Mr. Maxwell and our well-meaning, altruistic teachers who sought to point us toward high aims and to build up our self-confidence, their message was corrupted by the reality of limitations (social, economic, and political)—societal limitations that we experienced in our daily lives.

I sat in classes beside some really smart students: Leona Shapiro, Maxine Lieberman, Phil Rosenthal, Monte Nichols, René Jácome, Judy Fink, Gary Lemel, and Deanna Meyerson, to name a few. They were scholarly and disciplined students who took school seriously and who raised the bar to high levels of achievement. Competing with this bunch, as it turned out, was the best thing that could have ever happened to me. It prepared me for the world I was to inhabit later on in my life—a world that I could not even dream of just yet.

Maxine talked of becoming a doctor, Leona was politically inclined (and later became a state congressional representative in California), and René and Deanna's families owned large department stores. Presumably, they would inherit the family businesses one day. Lacking continuous, purposeful, exposure to dynamic family and community lifestyles such as those a majority of the Mansfeld students enjoyed, the average black student of the same age from Dunbar was slow to develop the desire to take risks, assuming the desire evolved at all. Though our education seemed adequate to us, a type of hesitance to venture out, a subtle form of caution persisted within the community that held ambition in check for most.

There were some notable exceptions—individuals who broke through the barriers of ongoing Jim Crow constraints to achieve high levels of economic, political, academic, and social attainment. Among them were Cressworth and Donald Lander; Laura and Jack Banks; Earl and Ruby Norsworthy; Edward Franklin Sparks; Joel Turner; his sisters, Sadie Turner Pitts and Anna Turner Jolivet; Olivia and Marlon Guess; Minnie Andrews; and Tommy Scott, to name a few. Former Dunbar students point with pride to the achievements of these individuals, for they are proof positive of the power of indomitable human spirit. All things really are possible to the courageous.

After graduation, we would transfer to Tucson High. It was one of the only three high schools in town, and it was definitely the largest. These new Mansfeld classmates and friends would soon be added to the old friends from Dunbar who had either stayed behind at John Springs or gone on to other schools near their homes. We would all attend the same high school. It had been two years since I'd gone to school with the Dunbar kids. A rude awakening awaited me when we rejoined each other

Tucson High School

Right away, trouble started when two former Dunbar girls threatened to beat me up in the hallway of Tucson High. The girls accosted me, alleging that I "thought I was white" because I had gone to school at Mansfeld. They accused me of being stuck up, and their intention was to put me in my place with a good butt kicking. Rosetta and I were together when this happened. She was a true friend in every way. Once we reunited at Tucson High School, she stuck by me every day. We ate lunch together. She supported me when I ran for office on the high school's student council, and she took up for me when this troublesome episode erupted.

Knowing what a poor fighter I was, Rosetta positioned herself between the girls and me, took off her coat, put her books on the floor, and told them in no uncertain terms that they would have to whip her first. Realizing that this would be a more formidable feat to accomplish, the girls decided to back down. I breathed a huge sigh of relief.

My extracurricular interests in high school gravitated toward things of a political nature. Although I was not very talented at modern dance, I was inducted into the Terpsichorus dance organization. I had had no formal training and had not studied styles such as ballet or tap, so my performance was generally stiff and perfunctory—not at all entertaining. I was, however, good at representing my sophomore class in student council meetings. I was a member of the National Honor Society, and, I had been secretary of student council at Mansfeld in the eighth grade. I knew *Robert's Rules of Order* and could draft proposals for changes in bylaws, codes of student conduct, dress codes, and other ordinances that guided life at Tucson High. We were not allowed to wear shorts, halter-tops, cutoff pants, or other of the myriad of clothing options that I observe on school campuses today. I enjoyed opportunities to present my point of view and listen to those of others. Now and then, my picture would turn up in the local newspaper as a member of the council.

Eventually, involvement in these activities caught the attention of some outside community leaders, and I was nominated by the black Elks organization to participate as a delegate to Arizona Girls' State in the summer of 1955. I was selected and went through the prestigious program, in which I attained the office of Mayor of the mock city of Saguaro, and was named one of three outstanding mayors of cities. The experience of living with girls similarly selected to the program from around the state of Arizona was phenomenal. I was one of two black girls in attendance that year.

The program was designed to develop civic consciousness, pride, and political skills in Arizona's future leaders. We set up a mock society and government, ranging from cities with councils and mayors to a make-believe state legislature, complete with a governor who was elected by the participants at the end of the two-week program. I had the good fortune and honor to be elected mayor of my little city, Saguaro. Rosetta didn't go with me to the University of Arizona for that experience, but I told her all about it when I returned home.

-Can You Say Boys?-

Aside from protecting me from prospective bullies at school, Rosetta helped me sort through many a decision; including which boys would make suitable boyfriends and which definitely would not. I didn't always follow her advice, but, I must admit, she was usually right.

No one from Dunbar would believe any of the rest of this story if I didn't mention Bill Newton. He was my first serious boyfriend. This will be a short story—perhaps the shortest one in the book. The long and short of it is that we were crazy about each other—in Bill's case, a little too crazy! A fact that I'm not proud of is that he frequently beat up unsuspecting boys who dared talk to me within his view. He was strong and muscular—he could (and *would*) hurt you. When he beat up a really nice guy who took me to a dance at school after he had joined the Marines and gone to San Diego to boot camp, my father laid down the law; I was *never* to see Bill Newton again! That was the end of that.

Dating in high school was like fishing through a hole on a frozen lake; there were few "fish" to be hooked, and a girl could take a tumble for the wrong guy and lose out on a happy life. Conversely, there were a few really nice boys, but none of them seemed to like me. After a few bad eggs and a couple of near misses, Rosetta, my other great friend, June O'Kelley, and I began dating older guys, airmen from nearby Davis Monthan Air Force Base. If the "frozen lake" was treacherous, dating airmen was like fishing in a very turbulent sea in a small raft. We had no idea what we were doing!

Eventually, however, Rosetta married her airman and gave birth to twins. June and I began double-dating two very different *men* (they were several years older than the high school boys we were used to), best friends, who were from large, urban areas—one from New York, the other from Michigan. The experience changed me forever. I suspect it changed June too.

-Keith Lockhart-

Keith Lockhart was about as different a person as I could have ever imagined getting to know…especially as a boyfriend. He had grown up in a middle-class family in New Jersey and had completed a degree in journalism at New York University. He was twenty-two years old and a second lieutenant when we met one night at Jack's Barbecue café. Jack's place was the central hang out of Tucson's black youth. In fact, it was the only place to congregate for social interaction—dancing, talking, flirting, playing music on the jukebox, and generally enjoying our youth and each other—other than Esteban Center, a city-owned recreational facility that included a dance hall, game room, outdoor sports areas, and the only swimming pool for black citizens.

I don't know what attracted Keith to me, but it was *awe* that attracted me to him. He was impressive, if not exactly handsome. Tall and dark, Keith displayed a style that I had never seen in a black man: he wore Brooks Brothers' ivy league clothes, drove an English-made MG car, and blew a trumpet. He also had his own apartment in town that was furnished nicely. Keith loved jazz and owned a substantial library of albums featuring all the famous artists of the day: Miles Davis, Thelonious Monk, Nina Simone, Oscar Peterson, and Sarah Vaughn, to name a few. I learned to love the sound of jazz through the exposure he afforded me. It was a classic, though not ideal, "east-meets-west" relationship.

At the end of my junior year in high school, I elected to move to Los Angeles to join my mother, who, thanks to the kindness of her friend, had made the move to LA, leaving Mr. Hill and his violence behind. My move was in part to reunite with the mother that I missed so much, and in part to get far away from Keith.

The difference in our ages was becoming problematic. He began to talk about sex, marriage, and kids. I was seventeen, and those were scary notions. My head swirled with confusion. I was deeply infatuated with Keith, and his persuasive personality could have easily won me over had I not left. He was distressed over my decision. At one point, after I had gone to Los Angeles, Keith and his friend drove to LA, and he found me and begged me to return. On the way back to Tucson, he wrote one of the most poignant letters I've ever received. In it, Keith told me that he was afraid I would "change too much" if I stayed in California. He implied that this would not be a good change, that I would somehow become corrupted by the glamour and glitter of a culture that was frivolous and fake. He wanted me to return to Tucson to "preserve the innocence" of the person he knew and cared for.

Although I've seen Keith only once since then, I've often thought about his concerns and wondered to what extent it was proven to be true. I know I changed. I changed a lot. But I called it growth.

Part III

Life in LA:
My City by the Sea

Cherish your version of your dreams as they are the architects of your ultimate achievements.

—Napoleon Hill

The California Dream

I have learned from reading and watching documentaries on the subject that the late forties and fifties were a time in U.S. history when Negroes moved out of the rural south in massive numbers and migrated to the west coast where they found great economic opportunities: plenty of work, lucrative wages, and the chance for home ownership and education for their kids. Many settled in Southern California, where the movie industry absorbed their skills. They cooked, cleaned houses, drove limousines, and provided personal care services. In Northern California, there was a boon in civil defense work. The war had opened opportunities for assembly line work and restaurant and shipyard employment. It was "Mecca": an ideal climate, sufficient money, and freedom—all in one place.

My brother, Carl Jr., joined the navy after dropping out of school in Tucson. By the time I moved to LA, he'd been stationed in San Francisco for some time. Most of his adult life played out in that part of the country, mostly in the city of Oakland. Cultural influences embedded in that community shaped his adult character.

Mama, now divorced from Mr. Hill, married for the third time the second year she was in Los Angeles. This time she married John Faulk. They had been neighbors and classmates as children growing up in Texas. He had secretly harbored a childhood crush on her, but she had never thought of him romantically back then. Neither had any inkling they would ever meet up again after they both left Texas. He'd gone to California where he was stationed in the navy. He subsequently married a California woman, had three children (Florence, Carmelita, and John Jr.), bought a home in San Pedro, and stayed. When he and Mama met up again through mutual friends, his marriage was ending, and she saw him in a different light. They began seeing each other socially, and soon the romantic sparks were flying. Within a year, they were married.

The couple made significant economic progress together. She worked as a waitress and sold Tupperware to earn extra money. Together, they bought the two-story duplex that became Mama's home for the balance of her life. The property was located in an area of Los Angeles that, at that time, was considered desirable. It was on what was called the west side. The house was not a showpiece by any stretch of the imagination; the floor plan was a nightmare by today's standards, it sat on a brick foundation, and the one downstairs bedroom was very small. The sale price, however, was perfect—it was a mere twelve thousand dollars! It was here that Mama, given her humble starting point, planted the first seeds of her remarkable accumulation of personal wealth.

In time, she expanded her potential to earn by studying real estate and, once she was hired, became a top salesperson in a prestigious realty firm in Inglewood, California. She sold many of the high-priced homes in the Baldwin Hills, View Park, Inglewood and Ladera Heights sections of LA. Though tempted, she never moved from her modest home on Gramercy Place. Instead, she and John bought two other income properties and succeeded in paying them off.

The couple, who had known each other since they lived on adjacent farms in Neylandville, Texas, grew apart after twenty-five years together, and, eventually, went through a bitter divorce, Mama's third. Originally, it had been a friendship recaptured. After all the dust had settled, I think that part, somehow, remained in place. It was a sad day all around when this dissolution happened. My brother and I liked Johnny, as we called him. He was the only granddad my children and his ever really knew (Daddy lived far away in Arizona), and he was my then-husband, Ken's, best friend.

When Johnny died, several years later, Mama was very sad. They had accomplished a lot together.

In regards to my brother's California life, distance from LA was both a blessing and a curse. In some ways, Mama and I liked it that way—what we couldn't see didn't bother us. Junior rode motorcycles dangerously fast, courted women of questionable repute, and generally developed a flamboyant lifestyle. We just left him to his own devices (or *vices*, if you will) always hoping he'd change his ways some day and return home.

He stayed with Mama for a time after he broke his collarbone in an accident in which a car he was working on fell on him. She patiently nursed him back to health, but he headed back north again as soon as he was able to travel. He had friends there, and he and Mama did not always see eye-to-eye. They argued a lot. He didn't expect to return.

That day finally arrived, however, in 1989, when our Aunt Rosetta, with whom he had been staying in Richmond, California, died. Displaced and without a steady income, Junior opted to move to LA to live with Mama. When asked why, he will state that she was getting older and he felt that she needed him to take care of her, but I suspect that the opposite was closer to the truth. He has never left either LA or her home since.

-Manual Arts High School-

Once I moved from Tucson to Los Angeles, my life took on a new and rapid pace. I entered a whole new paradigm of thinking and living. I went to work at my first public job. I was a part-time counter waitress at Von's Market in the Baldwin Hills Shopping Center, where my mother was also employed. After attending summer school at Los Angeles Senior High School, I enrolled in Manual Arts High in the fall as a senior. The school was known for its outstanding athletic program—it was a school full of champions. Trophies adorned the shiny hallways, and school spirit was sky-high. Unlike Tucson High's attendees, the student body was very diverse; there were whites, blacks, and Asians in, seemingly, equal numbers. Hispanics, in that day, however, were the minority group.

School life was fun. Amid the usual frivolity of youthful campus activities, there was a strong emphasis on academic work. I enjoyed the social atmosphere here, too. It was far more open and balanced than anything I had experienced before. I was the new girl in town who talked with a funny accent (they thought I talked "proper"), but I didn't feel at all inferior. I readily assimilated into the "in crowd." Unlike Mansfeld and Tucson High, I had no problems on the dance floor; boys of all races clamored to sign my dance card. Acceptance and popularity felt good. It was nice to live in a much more exciting social and academic climate. I thrived on the challenges presented by this situation. I was grateful that Dunbar and Mansfeld had prepared me to compete.

I soon became managing editor of the school's newspaper, The *Daily Toiler*, or just *The Daily*, as we called it. My taste for journalism was created in this role, and it was nurtured by a marvelous journalism teacher, Mr. Walterhouse. I was fortunate to work with a brilliant student editor named Carol Gilson. Carol was a petite, studious, white girl whose soul was wed to the school newspaper. My passion for writing was born right there. I learned to read upside down in order to manually typeset the galleys of pages of the newspaper. It was a skill I would use over and over in the teaching profession while reading stories to young students. That way, they could see the pictures as I read out loud.

The early-morning schedule I had to keep (I would arrive at 7:00 a.m.) in order to "get out the news" placed me into virtually all of the core academic classes with the school's jocks. They came early in order to get out of classes in time for long afternoon practice sessions. What a kick—one or two girls with all of the schools top athletes! There was never a dull moment in classes with the likes of Irwin Evans, Vance Irwin, Bobby Taylor, Bernard Mouton, Raymond Wren, John Golden, and Sam Joyner. It would take another volume to describe the feast of fun that took place in those classes on a daily basis. Words like: *raucous, insane, hilarious, delirious,* and *camaraderie* come to mind. In short, attending those early morning classes was a special, most memorable experience—especially Mr. Bland's chemistry class. When he handed test papers back, they were folded four ways: once if you got an A; twice if you got a B; three times if you got a D and in a wad if you failed the test. Vance received the most wadded up papers, but I probably ran a close second. Laughter and playful banter could be heard all down the hall every Monday morning following Friday quizzes. Mr. Bland tried to keep a solemn face, but any fool could see how much he loved his job. It was fun work, and we were fun kids. And, yes, we did learn the periodic tables.

One day, in our last period class, English, a memorable event took place. We heard a commotion outside the classroom in the hall. Suddenly, a short, slight-built white boy burst into the room. He wiped away blood from his bleeding lip as he stammered something about some big boys from another school who had entered the hall and hit him. He was a student "safety" who had been assigned to sit by the door to check hall passes.

All at once, the entire class of athletes went into action! They jumped out of their seats and bolted out of the room in search of the intruders. The chase, which I joined in order to capture the story for *The Daily*, led us out of the school yard and into busy traffic at the intersection of Santa Barbara Avenue (now Martin Luther King Boulevard) and Vermont. How we managed to cross the street without anyone getting run over, I'll never know, but we caught the guys trying to scale a fence beside Bank of America and dragged them back to the vice principal's office. The excitement of the chase stayed with me all my life.

It wasn't long after school started that I met and became attached to a charming, affable junior classman named Fred "Smooth" Taylor. We adored each other, and we were very compatible in spite of the slight difference in our ages. We went everywhere together; we even dressed in look-alike shirts that I sewed on a sewing machine I had won by answering a question on a radio show back in Tucson. It was cute—high school sweethearts. We were an item on campus—that is, until I graduated that spring and went to college, leaving Smooth behind at Manual Arts.

-College Days, Coed Ways-

I attended Los Angeles City College (now called LA Community College) for my first two years of postsecondary schooling. It was a good choice for one who was making so many transitions in rapid succession. College demanded a lot of me—ultimately, that I drop my ties to Smooth. Right away, I got involved with a contest being sponsored by a fraternity. If chosen, I would not be allowed to have Smooth escort me to the ball. I opted to participate and to be escorted by one of the frat brothers—a decision I would regret for its effect on my relationship with Smooth. He was not at all amused. His disap-

pointment struck a deep chord in me. I was torn between going on
to coed life and hanging on to my high school days. I couldn't have it
both ways, and it seemed unfair that I should date other people unless
he could also. I suggested we try that, but it was an unsatisfactory
solution for him.

Leaving Smooth behind made me sad. It turned out to be fatal to
our relationship, as well. It was a loss that was hurtful to both of us,
but life went on. We never hooked up again.

I received two five hundred dollar scholarships that helped me with
the cost of tuition and books. At LACC, I was exposed to opportunities to explore interesting courses such as philosophy, anthropology,
and public speaking. And I had one more shot at passing geometry
with a grade higher than the C I'd earned in high school. This was
important to me; I longed for a decent grade in at least *one* math
subject within my lifetime. My competition this time was a classroom
full of serious-minded returning Korean War veterans. They made
getting my coveted A pretty tough. I had to settle for a B.

I also had the opportunity and good fortune in junior college
to lead a prestigious women's honorary organization, the Alethians.
Membership required the recommendation of at least three faculty
members. I was one of two black members. I was voted president of
the sorority in my sophomore year. Presidency was quite different
from being a secretary. There was a lot more responsibility for the
ongoing success of the organization, and it was up to me to keep
people engaged in setting attainable goals and motivated for service.
I learned the meaning of collaboration and collegiality. My tenure of
one year was successful.

In addition to living a more expanded academic and social existence in a college located where sun, sea, and glitz were readily acces-
sible, I was also introduced to my life's work: teaching. It was due
to a summer job on a school playground that last summer at LACC
that I decided to pursue a degree in elementary education. I had
always loved children. Having an opportunity to work with them
on a daily basis, thanks to the LA Department of Recreation and
Parks program, solidified my resolve to make educating children my
career. I started as an assistant coach on a summer playground at
Normandie Avenue School in South Central LA. The playground

was the only place for most of the inner-city kids in the school's neighborhood to go to have fun during the summer. Due to their economic circumstances, they would not be going on family vacations out of town, and they would only get to go to Disneyland on a bus excursion with me, if at all.

It was my first real exposure to urban poverty; and it was a very different kind of poverty than I had known. This type of poverty had deep, insidious, roots. It was not just economic; it had a strong psychological component, and it was concentrated in pockets of humanity that stretched over dozens and dozens of blocks within the city limits of LA. One had to go a long way just to get to the outer perimeters of this zone, a journey too many of my kids would never take. A longing to change these conditions crept into my consciousness and gripped my very soul. It has never gone away.

At the conclusion of the summer program, I was promoted to the position of coach and assigned to supervise the after-school playground at Sixty-First Street Elementary School, which was located about five miles south of Normandie Avenue School. This was the first job in which I felt the weight of real, grown-up responsibility. At any given time after school let out, on any given day, there might be two to three hundred children in my care. The playground became my laboratory of sorts. Managing schedules, keeping track of materials and equipment, as well as enforcing playground rules and discipline were good primers for what was to come in the work I would pursue for a lifetime. I learned to build relationships and to both nurture loyalty in others and practice it myself.

I am reminded of the time when a stocky kid we'll call B. W., who was a first-class school bully in the sixth grade, challenged my authority to put him off the playground for starting a fight with another kid. He swore at me loudly, using filthy epithets, and he refused to leave. After a tense battle of words and threats, I put my red visor cap on the ground, handed my keys to one of the students, and picked B. W. up and carried him to the gate. He kicked, hit, and bit me every step of the way. Suddenly, five high school-aged boys who frequently played basketball on my court came up from behind and grabbed B. W. out of my arms and ran out the chain-link gate to the street with him. With a thud, they deposited his stunned body onto the sidewalk and warned him not to return or they'd give him more trouble than he could handle!

The whole playground of kids had gathered to watch the excitement; I couldn't afford to lose this battle with a toughie who everyone else feared. As a young female, I needed to assert not only my authority but my ability to back it up. Aided by my five loyal friends, my credibility was established that day once and for all.

-Jay* the First Time-

Toward the end of my sophomore year at LACC, something strange happened. I went to a Christmas party at the Kappa's fraternity house on a date with one of the local college guys, Ted Alexander. While standing on one side of the room, I spotted the very familiar face of a guy named Jay, from Tucson. He was wearing an air force military uniform, but I'd have known him anywhere. We had been good pals back home. He and his brother often gave me a ride to high school from my grandmother's house. We laughed and joked a lot on the way. He had even taken me out to a movie or a dance or some activity a time or two. Here he was in Los Angeles! We saw each other at about the same time, and we called out our respective names above the noise of the crowd and rushed toward each other. He swept me up in a grand hug. It was incredible—Jay...here! After a lot of hugging and babbling, we decided to leave the party (and my date) to go home while my mother was still up so she could see him.

We talked for hours at the kitchen table long after Mama retired to bed. When Jay left, he promised to write. Well, write he did. Letter after letter arrived at my house; each was more romantic than the last. Eventually, he asked me to marry him and move to Texas where he was in flight training. How flattering! I liked Jay a lot, but *marriage?* Well, I just wasn't sure.

"Let's talk about this face-to-face," I said.

"How about during spring break?" he suggested.

We agreed, and he sent me an airline ticket to Waco, Texas.

When I arrived in Waco, I had no idea what I was in for. I'd lived in a military town all my life, but I had not spent any time on the base. I had no reason to do so. Going through gates and having people saluting my escort at every turn (he was a second lieutenant) was an awesome experience. We also dined in the officers' club, using linens and silver reserved for the elite. I stayed in a suite in the guest quarters that Jay had reserved for me. One night, he dropped me off after dinner and sped away to some important meeting. I went to open the door that I thought was mine. I tried and tried to make the key fit, but the door wouldn't open. It was late, and I didn't know what to do. Just then, a very sleepy colonel opened the door wearing his boxer shorts. I had awakened the visiting grand pooh-bah who was there to inspect the base! He graciously let me know I had selected the door next to mine, the wrong door, and closed his. I shook for an hour. It was only one in a series of awkward moments that took place during the week I was there.

When it was time to leave, Jay placed a small diamond ring on my finger and said we were engaged. I liked how that sounded, but I still had doubts. When I got home, I sat on the couch and looked at the ring for a long time. I told Mama, "I'm sending it back."

And I did. Once I got back to the familiarity of my home and family, I realized how far from my goals marriage to Jay would take me; there would be travels to strange places, children, and more of the military life that I had tasted oh so briefly. I wanted something different for *myself* before I went off into his or anyone else's world. I wanted to finish school and get my degree. I had to be the master of my own fate. I sent the ring back and that was the end of Jay (for then). He never wrote or called after that. However, destiny had not played her last card. Little did I know that we would meet again thirty-three years later...only to pursue the same theme.

University Days

-Johnnie Cochran-

I first met the now-famous and recently departed Johnnie Cochran at summer school in 1955 at Los Angeles High School when I arrived from Tucson to make LA my permanent home. He was enrolled as a regular student, but LA High was out of my attendance area, so we seldom saw each other during my first year there. We next met in 1956 during my first semester at Los Angeles City College. He was the Polemarch (president) of the LA chapter of Kappa Alpha Psi fraternity. There was a meeting of its members called to interview prospective candidates for the court of Kappa Sweethearts, and to select a queen who would reign over the annual Black and White Ball. I was invited to the interviews by Ted Alexander, a friend I had met at LACC. Johnnie was chairman of the panel that would make the decision.

I was leery of the negative potential of such a venture because, when I lived in Tucson, I had a bad experience with the fraternity. The University of Arizona chapter of the Kappas had tried to embarrass me when I accompanied a high-profile frat brother to a U of A Bachelor's Ball. Malachai Andrews (called "The Prophet" by his peers due to his affable but straightforward personality) was a super track star who enjoyed great campus popularity. The fraternity was sponsoring him in an all-Greek competition for the title of "Bachelor of the Year," and they wanted him to do them proud. For the sake of their image, the Kappas wanted him to take Suzanne Preston, a pretty coed who had lighter skin than mine and silky, wavy hair. This was important criteria for what was classified as beauty in those days.

Although I was only a second-year student in high school, Mal

Andrews had already asked me to be his date, and he wasn't about to back down. He threatened to go to California for that weekend and skip the dance altogether unless they yielded to his desire to take whomever he pleased to the event. He stuck to his guns and escorted me to the dance. The brothers formed a line along the walkway leading to the ballroom where the dance was to be held. When we arrived, they inspected me from head to toe. Mal and I strutted past them in silence, heads held high; he looked like a black prince in his perfectly tailored white dinner jacket, red cummerbund, and black slacks; I looked like a stately princess in my light turquoise, waltz-length formal with a white, strapless brocade bodice. The white lady my grandmother worked for had given me the beautiful dress, which she had worn only once, as a special gift for the occasion. I wore a rhinestone tiara on my head. We looked regal! It was an in-your-face experience for both of us. Though he did not win the title, Mal won a special place in my heart and my total respect. I'll never forget him.

At the interview in LA, a panel of young men sat in a long line facing me as I nervously tried to answer a battery of their questions that were designed to qualify, or, more accurately, disqualify me. Some of my answers, admittedly, were flippant. I had learned the art of kibitz from my Mansfeld friends. It kept the dialogue between the panel and me spicy, rhythmical, and dynamic. It also helped me to mask the nervousness I was feeling deep down inside; I hadn't forgotten that Tucson experience. I thought rejection was on its way to me. When things threatened to go off course, Johnnie aptly redirected the group. It was his skill at leading meetings that saved me from falling into a pothole that would have kept me off the court. Instead, I was selected as one of seven young coeds to be escorted to the ball in long, white gowns. For me, it was a great honor, considering that I barely knew any of the people who chose me, and I knew virtually nobody at the dance.

After that event, I only interfaced casually and occasionally with Johnnie Cochran for a while, and then we saw each other much more often at the University of California at Los Angeles (UCLA) in 1958 after I became a student there. We encountered each other in the buildings' corridors or in the back of the student union cafeteria where black students gathered to eat and play cards. Johnnie's field was pre-law; mine was education. We had no classes together. Once in a while, we would attend the same off-campus house party. He was always friendly and cordial, but he never *actually* asked me to dance, either. Johnnie's demeanor was always affable, calm, and cool. He was smart and sophisticated, and he was the consummate gentleman to boot. I knew he would do well in life. I just knew it! I was right. In his lifetime, in spite of a background very similar to mine, he flew very high.

What I didn't know was the path that destiny would lay before him; nor did I know how, somehow, his path would intertwine with mine. In the years that followed, Johnnie was thrust into the forefront of a number of history-making legal confrontations: the Deadwyler case that precipitated the Watts Riots in 1965, the O. J. Simpson "trial of the century," and the freeing of Geronimo Pratt, UCLA classmate and brother of my great college pal, Charles "Chuck" Pratt. His freedom was secured after over twenty-five years of false imprisonment. Johnnie would not only do well; he would achieve greatness.

The last time I saw Johnnie Cochran, ironically, was in Austin, Texas, my new hometown. He was the keynote speaker at a MLK scholarship event at UT-Austin. He was startled when his eyes met mine among the crowd that gathered around him after his speech. "Shirley Robinson!" he shouted above the noise. "What are you doing *here?*"

We caught up briefly during intermittent spells of relative quiet while he signed autographs in the building's basement. It had been well over thirty years since we had been in the same place together. He thought I looked young; I thought he looked both youthful and classy, as always.

Last year, this friend and champion of justice left this earth to spend eternity in another realm. He was only sixty-eight. I will sorely miss him. It was always a source of comfort to believe that if I ever needed good legal counsel, I knew Johnnie Cochran—one of the best defense attorneys in the world.

-Bob Farrell-

I met Robert Charles Farrell in my senior year at UCLA. He was a short, serious, friendly guy with curly hair and a charming smile. His short physical stature belied the great store of bold ideas that he held in his head. His conversations with me were brief due to our class schedules, but they were intense. We discussed politics, philosophy, and ethics. He was a navy vet with familial roots in Louisiana. Compared to the other campus guys, he was refreshing. At the time, he was like a casual acquaintance who I never expected to gain significance in my life. As it turned out, he would later become a pivotal person, whose impact still reverberates. He would become my boss, and he would introduce me to my second husband.

-Jo Stanchfield-

Although I had many good teachers, the most significant teacher in my college life was a professor of elementary curriculum at UCLA, Dr. Jo Stanchfield. Dr. Stanchfield cornered me one day and set me straight in a manner that I'll never forget. Frankly, I didn't think she had ever noticed me in the class of one hundred fifty-plus students. But one day, she summoned me to her office to get a paper containing her critique of a learning aid I had turned in as a class project. I expected to receive praise and accolades for the beautiful artwork that I had stayed up all night to complete. Instead, I got a tongue-lashing and a dose of forthright reality, the likes of which I had never received from any college-level teacher before.

From the outset of the encounter, I knew this professor was not to be messed with. Her demeanor was serious and assertive. She held up my game-board learning aid so I could see it. Her first remarks were awkwardly complimentary: "It's cute. The colors are pretty."

Then she lowered the boom: "But it won't teach kids a damned thing! What's more, they'll have it torn up within an hour after you put it out." She went on to say, "This is not the caliber of work that I expect out of you, Shirley. You can do better. I've seen what you're capable of when you put your mind to it. I won't accept this. I want you to find yourself a primary typewriter and get some chipboard and some laminated contact paper. Then I want you to sit yourself down and think of a learning aid that will be worthy of children's time and that will help them learn a skill that they need to know. What you've given me to grade won't do any of that. The best grade I could give you would be a D. You're a better student than that, and I know it."

She was Miss Hirleman all over again.

I was beginning to feel pretty badly. It was disappointing to hear such harsh criticism of what I'd thought was an overnight wonder. But the worst was yet to come. She told me to move in closer to her desk. She also moved her body closer toward me. Then, leaning in and placing her face on her hand supported by her bent elbow, she looked me squarely in the eyes and said in a much softer tone, "Look, Shirley, what you did was okay, but okay will not be good enough for the kids you're likely to be teaching when you leave this university. If you were going to be teaching well-to-do white kids who get a lot from their homes, I'm sure you would do well. They can survive mediocrity in teachers, and do so all the time. But the likelihood that you, a black teacher, will be assigned to such a school is very low. More than likely, you will be assigned to a school that is populated by predominately black and poor students in the inner city. That's just the way it goes. The *last* thing these students need is a teacher who is mediocre. Practicing mediocrity on such students will only cripple them and further obstruct their path out of poverty. They deserve better. I won't pass you out of my class unless you understand this. You're black, Shirley. You *have* to be better."

These last words of Dr. Stanchfield's stabbed me deeply right in the heart. Surely she wasn't talking to *me*! Surely she didn't think I thought I was anything other than black. It was 1960, and I was really clear about my ethnicity. My first response was indignation. How *dare* she introduce race into the topic of my project? Was I being graded on my *race*? Surely not!

But the truth of her premise, that I would likely be teaching black students who needed the best teachers they could get, was a more compelling posit than anything I could think of with which to counter. It was powerful enough to start hot tears flooding down my cheeks. I thought of all that I had gone through to get here, of all the dedicated teachers in my past whose hopes for me were high, not to mention those of my family. I was the first to *ever* attend college, let alone such a prestigious school as UCLA. Was I letting them down? Was Jo Stanchfield right? Did I operate from some standard other than excellence? For that matter, had *excellence,* in this setting, ever been defined for me before today? I worked in isolation. I had not studied with or worked on projects with other students in a dorm or elsewhere. I'd gone to classes, gone to work, and gone home. That had been the sum total of my college experience. I had never checked my work against that of others.

I was crying, not because I felt sorry for myself, but because I had been busted by this white woman who had blatantly told me the truth; I was ashamed. I had hoped to get by with my cute project, not worrying one whit about its efficacy. In other classes, that would have worked; not much was expected of minority students. This time, however, I had been rebuked. My head had been rudely turned around one hundred eighty degrees. I left Dr. Stanchfield's office shortly after that, but the pain of my embarrassment lasted a long time. I ached for days after that session with Professor Stanchfield. I also started over on the project and finally completed something that was worthy of my effort. I received an A and a big hug from my teacher.

Somewhere among my things, I still have that project. It serves as a reminder to me of one of the most important lessons I've ever had to learn: *excellence needs no alibi; it speaks for itself.* No one has ever again had to teach me to be a *professional* teacher.

Shortly after that incident with my education professor, and while I was still pondering the meaning of excellence, I was on my way to the bookstore from Holmes Hall when I chanced to walk up on two icons whom I think personified the term "excellence." There on the narrow path that led between the two buildings, I walked directly past, almost touching shoulders with, a young senator from Massachusetts who was aspiring for the presidency of the country. He was being escorted across campus by another young man who was already president of the UCLA student body. The senator was John Fitzgerald Kennedy; the student was Rafer Johnson, the Olympic decathlon champion. It was an epiphany. The contrast in their skin color was obvious to the eye; one was white, the other black. But the element that distinguished the two individuals, for me and others who saw them that day, was excellence, and we were acutely aware that excellence was colorless.

Student life at UCLA was punctuated by challenging coursework and unprecedented enlightenment, which took place at a rapid pace. It was the beginning of one of the most radical periods in American history: the sixties. Change, radical change, was well underway. In my classes, I learned facts that startled me. In sociology classes, I learned, for example, that there were only seven thousand black school teachers in the entire United States in 1958. And I learned that Sunflower County, Mississippi, spent only fifty cents per year on the education of its black students.

I argued vigorously with the professor about the veracity of one of his "facts": that preachers constituted the largest percentage of professional blacks in the country, followed by beauticians, barbers, and morticians. I spent hours on research that I hoped would disprove him. It was embarrassing to be a black minority where statistics such as those were being dispensed to white students. To my utter chagrin, I found no evidence to refute what he had said. We blacks had come a long way since the bondage of slavery, but we still had a long way to go. I knew I had to be one who forged ahead.

I was grateful for art education courses that gave me a creative outlet for some of the frustration I was experiencing in English literature and sociology courses. Hawthorne, Melville, Thoreau, Lewis, and others had gotten under my skin and into my spirit. I no longer wanted to accept Christianity at face value. My head spun with questions and doubts. Insight was simultaneously a blessing and a curse. Art was my refuge. I loved the self-expression I was afforded by learning to paint in watercolor, tempera, and oil. Dr. Dietz taught me to sculpt in vermiculite, a porous lightweight material, and to mold clay into forms that could be both abstract and lifelike. She liked my work and nominated me for membership in Phi Delta Kappa Honorary Society.

I shall never forget the purple and magenta papier-mâché mule my one college buddy, Chuck Pratt, and I stayed up all night making at Mama's kitchen table. It was so colorful and real-looking. We "cut up" and laughed throughout the whole night. We were up to our armpits in starch and tempera with newspaper and paper towel bits all over the floor and counters. It was such a kick. We were so proud of our creation. Release and pleasure were byproducts of that work. My talent for art was shallow, but, nevertheless, there. To this day, I enjoy a sense of aesthetic savvy. It has come in handy many times. I still paint watercolors and splash color all over my eclectic home.

❦

Jo Stanchfield's prediction that I would probably teach black, poor kids, turned out to be wrong. Ironically, I was to teach the wealthiest children in the city's school system. This came about, I'm convinced, by spiritual intervention. In some way, I will always believe it was connected to the Jo Stanchfield incident. I say that because after her dress-down session with me, I changed my attitude about the schoolwork that constituted the balance of my pre-teaching courses. I had something to prove—that I could qualify with the best of 'em! My enthusiasm for coursework became more and more focused on teaching and learning; it was genuine and clearly observable. I turned in good efforts in all my classes and earned a good name among the education school's faculty. As a result, I was recommended for two of the most coveted internships of that time.

First, I was assigned to University Elementary School (UES), UCLA's prestigious, privately funded research school, which contained grades kindergarten through sixth. It was located on Sunset Boulevard, on the perimeter of the university's campus. Students were handpicked from waiting lists to attend the school. It was both ethnically diverse and academically dynamic. Leading education theories were exploited and explored here, and renowned educators freely walked the halls on any given day. Madeline Hunter, a well-known and universally respected educator, became the principal while I was there. To teach here, even as a student, was a great honor. The experience shaped my instructional philosophy and strengthened my love for the profession.

Led by master teachers like Emily "Webby" Griffith and Penny Moss, my two outstanding training teachers, and others like them, students were immersed in exotic cultural studies in which they lived (as nearly as possible) the way people in other cultures lived at that time. They worked, played, sang, and administered governments as authentically as one could imagine. Every effort was made to make learning deep, authentic, and personal—including a fourth grade project in which students built a simulated African village consisting of several mud and straw huts right on the grounds of the school. Not only did the students make and wear real-looking African clothing as part of their study, they also learned to cook and eat authentic African dishes. A by-product of this type of open-ended, inquiry-driven learning was the shaping of very liberal social attitudes. Students were free to question and seek answers from many sources.

In addition to reading textbooks, students often learned from real people. One day, for example, our fourth graders received a very important visitor from the African continent: it was Kwame Nkrumah, president of Ghana. He arrived, dressed completely in native garb. He came in response to letters students had written. What a day to be remembered that was! It seemed incredible that all this could take place so seamlessly from grade to grade; beginning at the kindergarten level, our programs coherently and systematically connected and expanded upon knowledge, concepts, experiences, and skills as children progressed to the sixth and final grade of elementary school.

Many celebrities' children attended UES. Among my fourth graders were the likes of Melissa Montgomery, daughter of famed singer and television personality, Dinah Shore. And there was Judy Beerman, daughter of the well-known Rabbi Leonard Beerman, who presided over Brentwood's largest Jewish temple. Knowing these families became singularly significant in my next school assignment. That story unfolded as I moved on to teach—first as a student, then as a probationary fulltime teacher—at Bellagio Road Elementary School, located on a hilltop in prestigious Bel-Air, California, which was just on the other side of Sunset Boulevard from UES.

Most pupils who attended this school—except for a handful who rode a bus—did not walk; they were driven to school by chauffeurs. Largely because there were no sidewalks, even students who lived closest to the campus were dropped off by either parents or servants. Virtually all of them had maids, cooks, and chauffeurs attending their families. These were the children of movie moguls, real estate developers, and music stars of that day. They were also children of lawyers, judges, and doctors. Few, if any, really poor children were enrolled in Bellagio Road School. Occasionally, a child belonging to a student at the university would become an enrollee.

-Marilyn Kivel-

Although schools in the Los Angeles Unified School District were, technically, not racially segregated in the deliberate sense that Tucson's schools had once been, they were, due to economics and many not-too-subtle real estate covenants, just as entrenched in de facto segregation, which fell along racial lines. This school, Bellagio Road, was most definitely de facto segregated. There were no black or Hispanic students in here.

In fact, there had never been a black teacher...until I came along. Had it not been for the foresight and generosity of Marilyn Kivel, sixth grade teacher extraordinaire, I might never have been hired. Marilyn Kivel went to bat for me at the end of my second student-teaching assignment. She was my upper grade–training teacher during my assignment at Bellagio Road. We hit it off, finally, after a rocky beginning. I had started the assignment two weeks late due to illness and temporary hospitalization. She had discouraged me from starting at first; she said she would only be able to give me a grade of C, at best, due to lost time. I begged. I needed to get out of school, out of Mama's house, and on with my life. I'd take the C if I had to. She relented, and I began teaching in her classroom the last semester I was in school.

It was a love affair. I loved the kids, the work, and Marilyn. They loved me back. At the conclusion of my term, Marilyn Kivel gave me a grade of A-plus and asked the principal to hire me for the next school year. When she was told there would be no vacancy, Marilyn offered to take her long-overdue sabbatical leave of absence if I could have her slot. The principal, Ruth Ehrlich, agreed, and I was offered the position of probationary fourth grade teacher. I was stoked! It was a first, not only for me, but for the university and especially for future black teachers who were still in school.

The event did not go unnoticed. I would live in a fish bowl for a good while. I wanted to succeed; I was not interested in fame or notoriety, but I did want my work to significantly impact the culture of the school community.

One thing that I could not influence was the practice of housing discrimination in the residential areas surrounding the Brentwood campus. Bellagio Road school was just a few blocks across the street from UCLA, but, though I tried, I was unable to rent an apartment anywhere within miles of my new job. Once I was hired, I was anxious to secure my own place to live. I wanted to get out of Mama's house and live on my own like the adult I thought I had become. Repeatedly, I called about vacancies that were advertised in the newspapers. On the phone, owners and managers couldn't tell that I was black; I sounded white to them. They would tell me to come over and see their places, but when I arrived, one by one, they would tell me how sorry they were; someone had just beat me to it. It was no longer available. At first I believed them, but then I began to see a pattern emerging. I didn't know about real estate covenants that kept certain ethnic groups out of neighborhoods. Finding out about them this way both shocked and angered me. There were no Fair Housing Laws to protect me from these discriminatory practices.

One day, during a telephone call, I insisted that a female manager of an apartment on Sawtelle Boulevard assure me that no one else had rented the apartment I was interested in. I wanted to ascertain this before I left home to see it. She laughed and promised me that the apartment would be mine if I wanted it. "Just come on over," she said.

When I got there and she opened the door, her face fell a mile, but she played it off smoothly. She took my twenty-five dollar deposit, and we shook hands with the agreement that I could start moving in the next day. By evening, her story had changed considerably. She called me to inform me that ten of her tenants had threatened to move out if I moved in, so, regretfully, she would have to refund my deposit.

I was livid! Wasn't this California? This was not Mississippi, was it? I looked up the tax records and found out the owner's name and phone number. When I called him to report what had happened, to my surprise and dismay, I got no comfort. The owner was Japanese, and he informed me that he couldn't live there either. He just owned the place. Something was really wrong with this picture! I had no choice but to continue staying with Mama.

Into the World of Work

-Bellagio Road School-

Soon after I began teaching at Bellagio, one of the greatest challenges and most significant events of my life occurred. I still marvel at the naivety with which I stumbled into the professional crisis that could have spelled the end of my career no sooner than I had begun teaching. It was February 1961, and Martin Luther King was conducting a sit-in in a Montgomery, Alabama, bus depot. How I got tangled up in that all the way in California is quite a miraculous story.

On Wednesdays, we had "current events day" in my classroom. Children brought in news articles from newspapers and magazines to share with classmates so that they could inform each other about and discuss newsworthy topics occurring around the world. This was also American History Week, which all public schools celebrated, with an emphasis on the contributions of Abraham Lincoln and George Washington. Bulletin board valentines with Lincoln and Washington's pictures pasted on large, pink and red hearts decorated schools across the country.

On this particular Wednesday, a very quiet girl raised her hand, frantically waving to be chosen to come up front and share her current event. I was so pleased to see shy little Susan wanting to participate that I called on her first. What she shared was a front page photo of policemen hosing down and large dogs biting a group of black people in Montgomery, Alabama. At first, the kids were very disaffected and ambivalent at the news. But it was the loud thunder of Stuart Work's voice frantically shouting from the back of the room that jerked them into consciousness.

92

"You guys!" Stuart yelled. "How can you just sit there like this? Don't you hear what's happening? Don't you care? Why, what if Miss Robinson were in that bus station? They would be siccing the dogs on her! Wouldn't that matter to you? How would you like *that*?"

Stuart had said the magic words; he had *connected* his fellow white classmates to the black dilemma. They had forgotten that *I* was black and that it could have easily been me being bitten by dogs and kicked and beaten by people who neither knew nor cared who I was. Now it was *personal!*

The classroom erupted in what seemed like spontaneous combustion. There was instantaneous pandemonium. Their young, fragile senses just couldn't process the images that were entering their minds. Fourth grade children tend to be very loyal to their teachers; mine were loyal to me. Unbridled emotions erupted. They yelled, they screamed, and they leapt up on the desktops shouting:

"I'd punch 'em!"

"I'd kick their butts!"

"I'd kill 'em!"

My children were upset individually and collectively—almost beyond control. Everyone in the school could hear them. I ordered them to sit down, get quiet, and listen to me. Finally, they did.

What I told them was the truth. I told them that they were upset because they knew me well and couldn't imagine why anyone would want to treat me so ruthlessly.

"However," I said, "if you had been brought up in that Alabama environment and had been present that day at the bus station, chances are you would have joined the mean people who were abusing the black folks."

I captured a teachable moment to teach them the word *prejudice* and its meaning. They got it. They understood.

Then I told them how, back at Dunbar when I was their age, we not only celebrated American History Week with George and Abe, we also celebrated the contributions of black Americans such as George Washington Carver, Mary McLeod Bethune, Benjamin Banneker, Harriet Tubman, Nat Turner, and a host of others. I wagered a bet with them that they couldn't name anyone who looked like me whose contributions to America's history we could acknowledge during this special week, along with George Washington and Abe Lincoln. To my surprise, they named three: Ralph Bunche, Marian Anderson, and Jackie Robinson—all contemporary Negroes who had achieved prominence in their fields and often appeared on TV and in the news media. I was proud of my students, but I challenged them to go home and bring back the names of three more worthy black people from history. I could not, in my wildest imagination, have imagined the trouble that would inure from that little innocent homework assignment!

The next day, parents started showing up in my classroom at 9:00 a.m. They brought visitor's passes. By noon, there had been at least twenty visitors and a photographer from *Time/Life* magazine had taken pictures of me in action with my students. I knew something big was up, but I didn't know how big it would be; I certainly didn't expect to be at the center of the movement that was sparked that day. What I didn't know was that there was a tight faction of John Birch Society members among my parents.

The Birch Society was an ultraconservative political group that operated out of concern for what they perceived to be a growing threat posed by the rise of communism in our culture. When these parents learned what their children had been asked to do for homework—which would mean taking the kids to libraries and discussing names of individuals they themselves had never heard before—they were very uncomfortable, and they came to see for themselves just who I was and what I was up to. They registered complaints with the principal. Mrs. Ehrlich was very nervous. She didn't know where to stand in the midst of this unexpected controversy that had drawn attention to her campus.

Admittedly, I didn't make things any easier for her; I steadfastly refused to review with her what I had said and what had taken place the day before in my classroom. Quite frankly, I felt insulted that I would be grilled about details of a social studies lesson I had taught. No other teachers that I knew of ever had to justify what they were doing in their rooms. Why me? When she asked me about the lesson, I defiantly told her that whatever I had said, I would say it again if the occasion called for it; I was not ashamed; nor did I feel any need to defend myself. I was a professional teacher, and I stood firmly on that distinction. She could have fired me then and there. I'm sure she contemplated it…but she didn't.

Instead, she called the PTA president, since the lesson and its fallout had turned into a community matter. The PTA president, believe it or not, was Mrs. Burt Lancaster, the movie star's wife.

-Norma Lancaster-

Norma Lancaster was an icon for liberal consciousness. She was a leader in community and civic affairs and the president of the League of Women Voters, and she had other similar involvements. When she came to my classroom before school started the next day, I had calmed down, and I felt safe enough to answer her gently-phrased questions and to share with her what had taken place the day before. Norma calmly listened to my side of the story; she had heard others' versions of events elsewhere. At the conclusion of our time together, she assured me that the problem was not mine—that it was a problem that had long been brewing.

"In my opinion," she stated, "these children at Bellagio are just as underprivileged as the children who live in south LA; they are not aware that there are many other types of people in the world because they have no opportunities to interface with them except in subservient roles. I think it's wonderful that they have a black teacher, but that's not enough. They need opportunities to play and work with peers, other kids, who are different from themselves. Otherwise, how will they ever be prepared for the world away from here when they grow up?"

She told me that she believed the situation needed to be changed. "And I hope to live long enough to see that it does!" she concluded firmly.

Norma's resolve—and that of other loyal community leaders like Rabbi Leonard Beerman and teachers like Webby from UES could not be matched by the Birchers, who had labeled me a communist and were demanding my ouster. Norma and the others went to work rallying the community against the ill intentions of that group. Thankfully, they were successful, and the Birchers' effort failed.

Shortly after this incident, it was my class's turn to present a program to the entire student body, and my students chose to perform a black history pageant. Stuart dressed up like a scientist and told the story of Dr. George Washington Carver's marvelous inventions and discoveries with peanuts and sweet potatoes. Another student, Lisa (whose last name I don't remember), dressed in a long, ruffled dress and a little white, frilly cap. She recited from memory all twenty-two stanzas of Paul Laurence Dunbar's beautiful poem, "When Malindy Sings" in flawless black dialect! We were bold and proud. My students had learned something that they would never forget; I was sure of it. Neither they nor the school would ever be the same.

I had married my college sweetheart during the winter break, but Ken, my new husband, was transferred to New York by his job. I stayed on to the end of the year when I resigned my position, regretfully, and we left for the East Coast. I've always wondered how many people believed I got fired…probably quite a few. But what I had started there took root and grew.

All summer, Norma Lancaster and a group of her friends held private cocktail parties and other fundraisers to secure enough money to charter a school bus to transport black (and a few Hispanic) students to Bellagio Road School from a school deep in South Central LA. They called their project, "Transport a Child." The first TAC students were, for the most part, the children of many of Los Angeles' "elite" black citizens: they were doctors', lawyers', and teachers' children, who came from middle to upper middle class homes. Some, however, did not. The children were bused from Normandie Avenue School, which was located at Vernon and Normandie Avenues. Theodore Alexander was the principal.

Results of the first year's efforts were so successful that other affluent schools in the areas surrounding Bellagio Road began to sign on for similar integration programs in which children were bused into their schools from the inner city. Soon there were as many as fourteen buses transporting minority children to the west side of LA for the purposes of educating them in previously all-white schools. Needless to say, the education effort went both ways—the white children and their teachers (who tended to be white also) benefited from the experience as well. Norma had started something. Actually, I like to think that my fourth grade class had started something—especially, my young, sensitive student, Stuart Work.

When the courts ordered LAUSD to exert more effort into eliminating de facto segregation in its school system, the school board decided to initiate a vigorous and massive busing program that would transport large numbers of students across town to effect what would be called "integration." There sat Norma's TAC program—a model of what could be achieved! Before long, the school district began picking up the cost of the program. It became their first busing program—one that was already in place. Ted Alexander (remember my date to the Kappa Christmas party?) was appointed to head the department that implemented what became one of the most extensive busing programs in the world, the Permit With Transportation Program (PWT).

Hundreds of buses and tens of thousands of (mostly minority) students began traveling out of the inner-city to schools that were not overcrowded and dilapidated, where the air was fresh, and school yards were not all asphalt; where green grass and pretty flowers landscaped the clean, modern facilities; and where highly qualified teachers were among the many educational benefits.

All of this has made a huge difference in the educational outcomes and career opportunities for thousands upon thousands of black and brown kids in Los Angeles. While I personally still believe in the neighborhood school concept, such as the one I participated in long years ago, I can't deny what integration of schools did for me. I guess my position on the subject today is: whatever it takes.

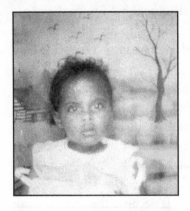

This is the only picture of me of a child that I've ever seen. I'm approximately two years old and rather dazzled by the camera.

This is my mother, Copply Williams Robinson when she was about nineteen years old. She was a mother of two young children. Wearing this hat, she looks quite grown up.

This is my handsome father at approximately twenty-six years old. He loved to sing in quartets in church. Maybe that's why he's so dressed up.

This is "Papa," my grandfather.
In my eyes he had no equal. He
was a great guy all around.

There were two "Big Mamas." This
one was my maternal grandmother.
The other one raised my mother.

This is a classic picture of Mr. Maxwell, Dunbar's principal, as I remember him: always businesslike. His powerful influence still resonates in my character.

This is a picture of the school that was so loved by its students, staff, and surrounding community. Paul Laurence Dunbar Elementary and Junior High School was the pulse of Tucson's black community when I was growing up.

One of the elements of pride shared by the Dunbar community. The Drum and Bugle Marching Band won many trophies for performing excellence.

This is a photograph of Mrs. Laura Banks and her husband, Jack Banks. She was my fifth-grade teacher. He owned the barbecue restaurant where all of us black kids hung out on weekends. It was the only restaurant where we could sit down to eat.

Election Winners

This picture shows me as an elected representative my first semester in high school. three of us were from Mansfeld. After attending school there, I could get elected to just about any office. There was not to be much diversity in representation in those days. I grew accustomed to being the token "first" and "only."

I was proud to be among the young ladies who were chosen by their peers to be mayors of the prestigious Arizona Girls' State. This experience further cultivated my appetite for leadership.

The Ariz
★ An Independent NEWSp.
TUCSON, ARIZONA, THUR: DAI

Mayors Of Girls State Cities

Five Tucsonans and one girl from Coolidge yesterday were elected mayors of the six cities in Girls State, which is currently holding forth at the University of Arizona. The girls and the towns they head are, left to right, Judy Fink, Salpointe high school, Ocotillo; Shirley Robinson, Tucson high, Saguaro; Sandra Smith, Coolidge, Manzanita; Joan Rews, Tucson, Chollo; Barbara Jackson, Tucson, Yucca; and Susie Stefft, Tucson, Palo Verde. Today's activities at State center around the nomination and primary election of county and state officials.

*My mother and stepfather, Johnny Faulk, whom Mama married
after moving to LA. They were married twenty-five years. He is the
grandfather my children knew best.*

Thelma Kleinerman was one of my parent volunteers in the Canfield-Crescent Heights School; I could spend hours talking with her. Here we are sharing thoughts after school while her daughter, Roseanne, and classmate, Beth Song wait.

Arthur Song (father of Beth Song) was a musically talented helper. Here he is teaching my class of third graders at Crescent Heights how to play "Jingle Bells" on flutophones.

Walter Young was a wonderful principal and mentor while I taught at his school. He and others led the way to the establishment of L.A.'s first alternative school for the purpose of eliminating de facto segregation. I am pictured here with him and his wife, Maxine, and parents at my going-away party. I was resigning to work at City Hall.

This is Robert Charles Farrell, the councilman for whom I worked after leaving teaching. He introduced me to the world of educational politics and to my second husband, Ernie Sprinkles.

My brother, Carl Junior, showed up to escort me down the aisle when I married for the second time. Here he is looking very dapper as he shares a laugh with Mama and me after the wedding.

This is the man who helped me alter the course of my life. Dr. Nolan Estes admitted me into the CSP Program at UT and guided me through to my PhD. His influence has been awesome!

This is my favorite picture from my trip to Europe. To me, it symbolizes my overcoming the odds to live a successful, triumphant life.

Mama and me showing our gratitude to each other for staying the course until we reached our goals. Her love and support kept me going.

My children and I in Mama's front yard after her funeral. It was a sad day, but we managed to smile.

*Our family at my daughter Ellen's Disney World
wedding. It was truly a magical time. Pictured
left to right: Jonathan Sprinkles, Kenneth
Brandon, Ellen and Cedric Calhoun, me, Caryn
Brandon, and Bruce Brandon (second row)*

*My beloved husband, Reverend Leo Morris.
He is my companion and friend for the rest
of this life's journey.*

This picture, taken in Holland, says it all:
I'm off to unknown destinations!

Part IV

Marriage and Family

*And God Almighty bless thee, and make thee
fruitful, and multiply thee, that thou mayest be
a multitude of people...*

—Genesis 28:3

First Marriage

-Kenneth Brandon-

Ken Brandon returned from four years in the United States Air Force and enrolled in UCLA to pursue the balance of his undergraduate degree in mathematics. He was tall and somewhat handsome, with a calm, laid-back demeanor. As I'd emerge from classes in Holmes Hall, I'd often encounter him standing outside taking his last smoke before entering the building for class. He always greeted me pleasantly, and usually struck up a brief dialogue with me before we parted. By the second semester of my last year, we had begun dating, if one could call it that. Neither of us had much money, so we either went to house parties or stayed at my house watching television and playing dominoes and cards with my parents (rather, Ken played the games; I was not so good at them, so I declined most of the time).

At school, we sometimes held hands…usually when we were well out of sight of the other black students. He didn't live on the campus either. Our romance flagged right from the start, though; it was anything but torrid.

I was drawn to Ken because he seemed older and more settled than the typical college males that I had encountered thus far. Besides, he paid *some* attention to me; the other UCLA guys, for the most part, did not—at least it didn't seem so. No one I was interested in ever asked me for a date. They tell me today that I always seemed so "serious"; they were scared to ask me out.

With less than one hundred black students in attendance fulltime (it seemed closer to fifty than one hundred), most of them females, the males could have their pick of girls to go out with; I thought that most of the girls offered much more than I: they had time, they were fun to be with, and they wore nice clothes. Some came from relatively affluent families where their parents were either professionals or well-paid civil servants. They lived in fairly prestigious residential locations in the Los Angeles area, such as Pasadena, Altadena, Windsor Hills, Baldwin Hills, View Park, and Ladera Heights.

There were others, like me, who lived close to Crenshaw Boulevard and even farther east near Watts. Those of us who didn't live in dorms on campus commuted to school in carpools. Ken lived farther southeast from my house with his mother. He drove his car and picked up riders in a carpool just as I did. The money they paid us paid for gasoline and covered our own transportation costs.

There were no railways, freeways, or even buses going to UCLA from where we lived, so it was essential that we knew what time it was and never missed rides to and from school. This circumstance made the socialization process very difficult. Because we worked off-campus and lived at home, we had virtually no time to partake in normal campus social life, to get to know people in depth, and to sort through potential future mates to select the best match.

In a sense, Ken and I were pushed together by this common "handicap." Our selection of each other as marriage partners was awkward, poorly timed, and, in retrospect, ill-advised. Neither of us had taken the time to know ourselves well enough to figure out what type of person would make the best lifetime mate.

Today, I have few memories of any particular dates that Kenneth and I shared during our courtship. There were no movies, no candlelight dinners, no flowers, no church activities, no picnics, no hiking, and no other getting-to-know-you activities that people ordinarily engage in prior to becoming permanent partners. There were, however, a few student-related club meetings that we attended together, such as a book club (in which we read and discussed *Black Bourgeoisie,* a new book about values and cultural practices of the so-called black middle class, which was published in the sixties), and there were NAACP meetings. Like his older brother, Everett Brandon, who graduated before we got to UCLA, Ken was elected president of the campus chapter.

I did have a few opportunities to meet his family before marriage, and he interacted with my mom and stepfather quite a bit. In fact, he and John Faulk, my mother's third husband, became very close friends over time.

On December 17, 1960, in Bethany Baptist Church, the wedding of two of the most unlikely life partners took place. My mother-in-law, Mae Brandon, a kind, gentle woman and a talented seamstress, sewed my beautiful white, sequined, lace dress. The small wedding party consisted of maid of honor, Billie Ray Cahill (my new best California friend); best man, Ellis Dickerson; and little cousin flower girl, Kathy Spigner. In addition to friends and family, in attendance were over four dozen fourth grade pupils and their parents. It was a very memorable day. We acted as if we were in love. I wasn't sure we really were. Time would test that.

The Brandon family had moved to Los Angeles from the Panama Canal Zone, as it was called in those days. There were five siblings. They were all bright and ambitious. All three of the boys, Everett, Clifford, and Kenneth, ultimately graduated from UCLA. Clifford played basketball on John Wooden's team, and Everett headed for law school at Hastings Law School in San Francisco. Betty and Sarah, Kenneth's two sisters, were both very artistically and athletically talented. Fitting into this family was a daunting challenge, one I felt throughout the duration of our marriage on one level or another.

-Speed Bumps in the Road-

While traveling across country in June 961, Ken and I encountered the first episode of blatant Jim Crow practice that I had seen since my youth in Tucson; we were refused service in a crowded roadside restaurant because there was a policy, enforced by the owner, of refusing service to blacks. I was shocked! It was 1961. How could this be? I was so indignant and irate that I wanted to stand on the tabletop and tell everyone seated in that restaurant why we were leaving. Ken pulled me out by the arm, preventing me from action.

"Come on, let's just leave," he said.

How could he be so passive about this matter? Didn't he feel the hot rush of anger and humiliation that I felt? It was my first hint that our personalities were destined for a collision course. I had become a warrior; I wanted to win this battle.

Ken was a realist and not at all confrontational. He realized that the battlefield was bigger than both of us; we couldn't win alone. "Let's go!" he insisted.

I stood there for a while seething. My mind kept flashing back over some of my most recent experiences; I had graduated from a very prestigious university, taught children of some of the most prestigious white families on the west coast, and won the respect of a whole community. I was good enough to do those things. Here, by contrast, I was not good enough to have a couple of pancakes while seated in this little restaurant among working-class white folks. It was humiliating, hurtful, and infuriating.

What saved the day for me was a courageous move on the part of a white man, a fellow traveler, who had witnessed the whole event. As we started to walk out, he gathered up his entire family—children, wife, and all—in the midst of their meal. He paused at the front counter and stated to the owner: "If they can't eat here, we don't *want* to!"

They went out the door behind us, got into their car, and left. I felt a lot better. After that, I removed the veil of colorblindness from my eyes. I guess one could say I activated my guard. I would never be caught off guard again by blatant racism.

As it turned out, we did not settle in Syracuse, New York, as planned. Instead, Ken requested and got a transfer to South Jersey. The climate was just a little milder there than in northern New York. We were both happy about that, but my dream of pursuing a master's degree at Syracuse University was lost in the change of plans. We moved to Trenton, New Jersey, where we met new friends, George and Betty McNair. They were our world for the time. George and Ken became close buddies. Betty and I bonded with each other nicely as well. Betty was a teacher, also.

I'd hoped to get a teaching job in the Trenton school system, but that plan was derailed by yet another episode of what I perceived to be blatant racism. When I went to the district's Personnel Office to be interviewed for a position that I had seen advertised in the newspaper, the personnel officer, a white woman with whom I was to interview, acted very indifferently toward me. In fact, she had not even read my application—which became obvious as we initiated a discussion about my qualifications. She was ready to dismiss me within five minutes of sitting down with me; she simply told me that all the positions had been filled. She rose from her chair and extended her hand in a farewell gesture, but I persisted in engaging her in conversation a little longer. Her demeanor changed markedly as we moved from topic to topic. She relaxed her rigid shoulders and offered me something cold to drink. My fluid speech patterns, good diction, and correct use of Standard English captured her attention.

Finally, she asked me where I was from. I directed her to the first page of my application. She then wanted to know where I had attended college. I pointed to the place in the application where that information was to be found. The interview proceeded in this manner until she had gathered all the facts about my qualifications. I could see visible embarrassment in her face. Without investigating what was documented in my portfolio, this lady had assumed I was someone else.

"I thought you were another of those poor little colored girls from the south. Bless their hearts," she said, "I feel so sorry for them when they come in here looking for employment. They are just not adequately prepared to meet our high professional standards."

Hearing these words sent a chill up my spine. She was clearly faced with a dilemma: this "colored girl" was a graduate of one of the most respected universities in the world. I was definitely not a poor little ill-prepared colored girl from the south. I was standing there, well prepared and available to work, but the district (according to her previous statement) had no room for me. I sat back in my chair and dropped my shoulders. The question that surfaced in my mind was *how had she known the girls who'd preceded me were not prepared?* Had the color of their skin disqualified them at the door, as it, apparently, had disqualified me? I was beginning to understand why there were so few black teachers. White institutional gatekeepers, like this one, could easily determine how many would and would not get hired. It was an awareness I had not expected to encounter here in the northeast. It was chilling! Was this not similar to what I had just experienced in New Mexico on my way to the east coast? Was this the waitress dressed up in a business suit?

After about a half-hour, we ended the interview, said polite goodbyes, and I left for home. By the time I reached our apartment, my interviewer had placed phone calls to everyone in our building. Our phone had not yet been installed, so she left messages for me to call her back. Miraculously, yes, "miraculously," a position had just opened and, "The district would be delighted to have Shirley fill it."

I did not call her back. My pride was badly bruised. The scab of rejection that I had felt at that restaurant in New Mexico just a few days before was still fresh.

"No way!" I said out loud when I heard the messages. My mind was made up.

The next day I signed a contract with Hamilton Township School District, located right next door to Trenton. I would become the only black teacher in Greenwood Elementary School, where, once again, all but one of my students would be white.

In retrospect, now that I'm older and have a more mature understanding, I realize how I sacrificed a golden opportunity in order to make an egotistical statement. I've often thought that I should have taken that job with the Trenton School District. I could have done so much to make things better for prospective black teachers by doing a great job and proving that color really did not matter. But I was young and impetuous. My ego, at the time, was greater than was my perspective. I could have been a Josie Daniels, Laura Banks, or Etta Jackson to so many of the African Americans who populated the student bodies of Trenton schools at that time. It was, indeed, an opportunity missed.

I taught only one semester at Greenwood due to becoming pregnant. In that school system, when one started to "show," she had to take maternity leave. This was disappointing to me. I was just getting used to working in the more traditional setting where there were basements and grass fields for playgrounds (though I was appalled to see that children with special learning needs were housed in the basement and not allowed to intermingle with mainstream students). I'm sure I could have learned a lot.

Our first child, Bruce, was born in Trenton in May of the following year. We lived in New Jersey for two and a half years. After that, Kenneth and I returned to Los Angeles.

Prior to leaving, our neighbors in Mount Holly (the small town near Trenton where we had moved to be closer to Ken's work) gave us a big farewell party. It was the most fun we'd ever had together. There was card playing, dancing, and drinking until the wee hours of the following day. Ken drank enough to loosen up more than I'd ever seen him. He was the life of the party. He joked with the guys (most of whom he'd never met) and generally entertained everyone with his jolly spirit. Because his demeanor was usually so quiet, the neighbors had never seen this side of him. Neither had I, but it was a welcome sight. We were going home, and we were both happy!

Reflections

Coming home was not at all like I had fantasized. I thought I would be so glad to get back to a more lively social setting—back with family and friends who would be delighted to see us. I had longed for my own home as we'd been living in an off-base apartment complex near Fort Dix-McGuire Military Base. I had made a few good friends there, but I'd wanted to go home to California. To my dismay, it took almost four months of cramping up in Mama's tiny front bedroom with my husband and toddler before we finally moved into our own first home—a brand-new, three-bedroom tract house, which Ken selected, that was located a few miles south of LA in what is now known as Carson.

It was there that family life really began in earnest for us. We had two more children (daughters, Caryn and Ellen), a mortgage, bills, a neighborhood social life, and a family-based support system. Some of my dearest friendships were kindled in Carson: Bettye Love, Miranda "Randi" Pratt, Georgia Brown, and Alice Fisher still live there. We took care of each other when our babies were born; cooked together; gossiped together; diapered, burped, spanked, and scolded each other's children; and cried together when life and/or our husbands dumped on us. Those women were treasures to me. No matter where I have lived since those days, I have always remained close with them.

As to Ken and me, our first serious marital problems (which occurred when I first discovered that he was having an extramarital affair) were born and grew larger in this place. I loved it, then I hated it, then I loved it, then I hated it...but mostly, it was *home*.

Abrupt Change

-The Watts Riots-

I had become complacent as a suburban homemaker, staying home for over five years to cook, keep house, and rear children, but the time came when I felt compelled to return to work as a school teacher. I might have been moving in that direction anyway, psychologically, as marital discord became more and more pervasive, but a single cataclysmic event pushed me into the definite decision: the 1965 Watts Riots rent South Central LA into shreds. The violent response of the community to perceived heavy-handed, unjustified harassment of a black man and his family members by law enforcement officers of the California Highway Patrol, brought home to all the seething unrest of a disenfranchised people who lived just north of our home. Twenty-eight African Americans were killed in the upheaval, and hundreds of businesses were burned to the ground. There was shooting and looting, and dozens of arrests. Emergency sirens wailed from every corner of the earth. For a few days, I thought I might actually be witnessing those "end times" that the Jehovah's Witness guy from my youth had predicted. I stood on the curb of my front yard watching huge, billowing, black clouds of smoke rising to the skies above Los Angeles. The city was on fire in a way that could only be described as the epitome of hell. Once again, my terror was all-consuming.

What was I to do? How could I prepare my family, which then consisted of a husband, two small children, and myself, to escape from what seemed like endless rage and destruction? And it seemed to be coming in our direction. This would surely be the end of *our* world...surely! The insurrection continued violently for nearly a week. This time, I was not sleeping outside; I could witness the unfolding

revolution that was taking place within ten miles of my home on television. Every nanosecond of air time was filled with reports of violent
acts, and rampant destruction and countless testimonies of despair. It
was an agonizing, gut-wrenching experience.

When it was over, I realized that people braver than I had initiated
precipitous action that got the rest of the world's attention and that,
yes, the world as I had known it had indeed come to an end. And it
had been cataclysmic and terrible. Was this the work of a guy named
Jehovah? I never found out. But I do know that when the ashes finally
cooled, a new world began to emerge for black and brown people
everywhere in America. Blatant racism and discrimination of all types
were uncovered and exposed to scrutiny and disclosure. There was no
place to hide. A new day was born for oppressed people of color—
first in California, then throughout the country.

These "end times" had led to the abolition of ignorance—ignorance about the plight of formerly faceless, nameless people whose
suffering had been taken for granted and tolerated for too long. Now
everyone knew the truth about California, particularly LA—that
there was oppressive racism here, too. That awareness was airborne:
telecast worldwide. The end of my world as a "Negro woman," I
realized, was here at last. The color barrier that I had struggled to get
beyond since I was old enough to recognize it was on its way down;
first, within my own consciousness, then, hopefully, in the outside
world as well. Black was no longer to be thought of as "ugly" and
inferior. A new proclamation being heralded throughout the world
was that "Black is beautiful!" I felt that I would no longer have to
explain myself to a white world or to "qualify" by being near-white
in my demeanor, speech patterns, and dress to be acceptable. Nor did
I have to straighten my hair and wear nylon hose that were tinted in
the light shades of white women's legs (as they mostly were in those
days). I was free to just be myself. I was reborn. My new life began,
not in heaven, but in a newly ordered world. I was renamed, black
American, and that was just fine!

The following year, in May of 1966, a similar incident involv-
ing a case of police brutality against a black man occurred. Leonard
Deadwyler was shot by police after being stopped en route to the
hospital with his pregnant wife. Once again the city teetered on the

verge of deadly, destructive eruption. Looting and burning started up again, but did not reach the proportions of the previous year. This was due, in part, to the swift action on the part of the city's district attorney, Evelle Younger, to authorize a coroner's inquest into the shooting death and to allow it to be televised. The family of the victim decided to sue for a judgment of wrongful death. Ironically, the brilliant young lawyer selected by the Deadwyler family to litigate their case against the police department was the outstanding young lawyer and public defender, Johnnie Cochran, my UCLA classmate. I was mesmerized and glued to the TV throughout the whole ordeal. He handled the case and himself masterfully. From there, his career took off for the sky like a rocket.

The daily images of frustration-gone-mad were too compelling for me to ignore. I thought of what Norma Lancaster had said about the Bel-Air children. Intuitively, I knew that underprivileged and poor children living in Watts deserved more than they were getting. Years of educational neglect and intractable poverty were now boiling to the surface. As a teacher, I had to respond to the call for help. There was no way I could turn my back on the situation that had been brought to my attention with consummate clarity. I hired a babysitter for my kids and applied for work in the inner city.

-Wendell Warner-

I was hired to teach sixth grade in Miramonte Elementary School, a Kindergarten through sixth grade school where, ironically, the principal was the same man who had hired me when I was in college to direct play activities on his playground at Sixty-First Street School. Wendell Warner became my second significant professional advocate. He gave me opportunities for leadership and singled me out for specialized training in courses such as Spanish Language Acquisition and multicultural awareness that provided texture to my career and assisted in my marketability as a professional bilingual educator in future years.

I'll always remember Wendell's shocked, somewhat dismayed reaction the day he saw me wearing my new Afro hairdo. He wasn't the only one. A lot of the teachers were surprised to see me expressing my "radical" side. I don't recall how or when I decided to let my hair go natural instead of processing it to straight. But I do recall how freeing it was to be my natural self.

I taught at Miramonte for six years. During that era, several federal educational entitlement programs were born. Among them were Title I[1] and Head Start[2]. The push to level the educational playing ground for children of poverty began in earnest, with some spectacular initial results. Training and staff-development of teachers was highest among the priorities. Fortunately, I returned to the field in time to partake of much that was offered. I will always be grateful for that.

What I didn't expect was the difficulty I would encounter managing the students. Discipline hadn't been the focus of my UCLA education. Educational theories had been stressed more than the practical aspects of classroom management. My first semester back in the classroom was tough…to say the least.

Culturally, there was a mismatch between my students and me—in spite of the fact that I was black like the majority of the students I taught. I found out in those first few weeks just how important language (and its interpretation) is. My students couldn't understand me, and I didn't always understand them. "What do you mean?" someone would ask whenever I'd issue an assignment for work, and I would often ask a child to repeat what he or she had said. I needed more time to understand their words.

"Teacher, you talk funny!" I heard many a student say.

I felt hurt and confused. What was wrong? Why couldn't I connect with these students with whom I thought I shared so much in common? For one thing, I didn't speak Ebonics, a form of Black English that has its roots in slavery but has evolved over time to be spoken, with modifications, almost as a primary language, by lower

1   Title 1 is a federal entitlement program that provides additional funding to support school-age students whose family income is at or below poverty level. Included in that support are free and reduced meals and certain supplemental educational personnel, equipment and supplies.

2   Head Start is a federally funded early-childhood program that targets four-year-olds. Its objectives are mainly to provide good nutrition, educational readiness activities and materials, and parental training and involvement to prepare preschool children for a positive academic, physical, and emotional start in grade school.

socioeconomic class blacks who spend most of their time in ghettos. Some think of it as "broken English"; but it is not. Ebonics is best described as "adapted" English; it combines dialects, vocabulary, and conventions of language that are widely practiced and understood by most of us who are descendants of slaves. It took my Tucson friend and scholar in the study of Ebonics, Dr. Hollis Armstrong, to explain this phenomenon of culture to me. I soon learned this new language—at least to understand it, if not to fluently speak it!

I had not factored in the impact of societal oppression that played a huge role in ghetto life: low aspirations; diminished, unrewarded effort; and fear of one's own people. Neither my perceptions nor my speech patterns had been shaped in this setting. They had been shaped in Dunbar, Mansfeld, and Tucson High. I was different, and my students knew it. I had been poor in my lifetime, true enough, but poverty here was not the same. I had been taught to have hope for a better day; it was drilled into me. "Just *try*," I was taught. And there were models of success within my view: businessmen, Creed Taylor and Tommy Scott, Sr.; the doctors Thompson, one a physician, the other a dentist; and all of my teachers.

Adjusting and moving from near-failure to ultimate success at Miramonte took time. I was determined to see it through. My six years were well spent; I prayed, and I grew. Wendell supported growth in my career by appointing me to key committees and selecting me for specialized training. He also assigned me to host the district's Program for Inter-group Education (PIE) in our school. The program involved pairing a class of our all-minority schoolchildren with a class of all-white students from another school for a monthly exchange. Once a month for an entire semester, my fifth grade class went on educational field trips to places like Marineland, the LA Botanical Gardens, museums, and the beach. PIE was intended to foster inter-group understandings and friendships. Without such a program, these students would never have had opportunities to interact with students of other races. Because of my background, I was a good ambassador for our school.

New Directions

Ken and the kids and I moved from Carson to Los Angeles when we sold our house; we'd planning to move to San Diego because Ken's job had scheduled an impending transfer there. The transfer fell through. But the house was gone, so instead we headed north a few miles and bought a small house in the Pico-Robertson neighborhood in west LA. This seemingly innocuous move evoked revolutionary change. First, I changed schools; later I changed careers; then I changed husbands.

When we moved, I transferred from Miramonte to a non-inner-city school in west LA near our new home that was led by a dynamic black principal, Walter Young. Integration was rapidly moving westward in the city, taking in the Fairfax-Robertson-Pico area where we had bought a home. This put me in position to be involved in establishing the first public alternative school in the Los Angeles Unified School District, Canfield-Crescent Heights Community School. Working with a different breed of parents whose involvement in educational matters was dedicated and well organized, I learned the meaning of parent power. These parents were not poor; nor were they black or Latino. They were white (largely Jewish) and affluent, reminiscent of the parents of my classmates' from Mansfeld, back in Tucson, Arizona. They were assertive, if not out-right aggressive. With them behind me, I personally confronted the school board to demand changes in delivery systems that had not yet been heard of in the inner city. We prevailed...always.

I'll never forget that first meeting of the Canfield-Crescent Heights Alternative School Task Force Committee. Tensions were so high in the small living room where we convened that you could cut the air with a knife. It was Clive Hoffman who had first stood up and proposed the idea of combining the two schools. Looking back, I realize just how

courageous an act that was for a well-to-do white man who had everything to lose if the plan backfired. Voluntary integration of schools
was a much talked about, but seldom implemented, ideal. Clive was
proposing that both blacks and whites in the two neighboring communities whose attendance boundaries were separated only by a busy
boulevard (Robertson) put their actions where their mouths were. For
months, the school district had conducted "dialogue meetings" to air
community and parental concerns about the impending court order
to end widespread de facto segregation. "White flight" was rampant in
communities targeted for busing. For Sale signs blanketed lawns and
sidewalks throughout large, white residential sections of the city. Every
excuse was used for getting out. But "Get Out!" was the unmistakable
theme of the exodus of the white middle class.

So here stood Clive, calmly welcoming the overflow group of fifty
or so anxious parents—half white, half black, who had accepted the
invitation to be part of the first alternative school in the LAUSD.
It was to be a school with a radical, pro-social mission: to provide a
melting pot educational environment for children from diverse ethnic
and cultural backgrounds. This was to be accomplished in a city that
was way over the edge in the progressive pattern of racial polarization.
Heaving chests were relieved by muffled sighs, which punctuated the
thickened air of the meeting room as the first timid comments were
presented spelling out the goals of the project: racial and cultural
diversity among both students and staff and an educational delivery
system that would be open-ended and nontraditional. Clearly, it was
going to be a long night, and it didn't take a genius to see that it was
also going to be a long journey from where we were starting to our
proposed destination.

As the weeks and months of wearisome planning wore on, evidence
began to emerge that designing a high quality, uncontrived, multicultural school setting was hard work. Widespread ignorance and paranoia
on the part of adults presented a formidable hurdle in the initial phases.
This was addressed by rap sessions (some quite heated) and fieldtrips
to sites where the group could observe success. One such site was in
San Francisco, California. Twenty parents, including myself, flew to
the site of the Multi-Cultural Institute (MCI), where we spent one
week visiting and observing classrooms for several hours at a time. The

school drew its enrollment from a cross section of Bay area children who were voluntarily enrolled by their parents. They came from virtually every ethnic segment of the city's huge, diverse population.

MCI was organized into ethnic and cultural classrooms: black students were placed with black teachers and studied a curriculum organized around an Afro-centric perspective. The programs of Chinese, Japanese, Italian, German, and Mexican children were similarly organized and staffed. The theme of the school provided the central focus of all instruction: "Different, but the same." In this unusual educational setting, students were deliberately immersed in studies focused on aspects of their own ethnic culture for long periods of time then dispersed to blend with the children from other cultures to share, compare, and appreciate discoveries they made about similarities as well as differences between their respective groups.

The daily rhythm of learning history, geography, literature, and art from an ethnocentric perspective was observably effective in establishing a solid sense of self and group identity in each student. One did not have to look hard to observe the depth of knowledge, understanding, and pride that characterized the experiences of the children. These elements were reflected in their products as well as in their deportment. Clearly, however, there was redundancy in the customs, rituals, and traditions that each group claimed as its own. Students readily deduced that, in spite of certain obvious differences, they were truly the *same* in many more ways than they were different. It was an awesome experience for all of the parents and teachers who made the trip—and an especially sobering one for me. I had thought such a pull-out program would constitute resegregation in a negative way, but I was won over by what I saw. It wasn't negative at all—it was very affirming.

After much hard work and the bridging of a wide chasm of mistrust, our taskforce produced one of the most comprehensive plans for voluntary integration that the city of Los Angeles, California, has ever known. Students in grades K–3 attended Crescent Heights (the previously virtually all-black) school; grades 4–6 students were assigned to Canfield (the previously all-white school). Since the distance between the campuses was less than a mile, parents formed carpools to transport the younger students, while older students either walked or rode bicycles. My children attended on each campus.

We developed an alternative curricular approach that would employ multicultural themes decided upon by the parents and teaching staff. It was different from what was available in mainstream schools in the district—very different.

Canfield-Crescent Heights Community School still exists. Although it has undergone many changes, it is still one of the vivid reminders of the powerful potential of ordinary parents to influence the direction of their children's education. As Norma Lancaster had, the parents and professionals involved acted on their belief that real world *socialization* was equally as important as test scores in their children's development.

-Walter Young-

I stayed on as third grade teacher at Crescent Heights School. Walter, who was the principal of both schools, liked my open-class-room instructional approach and my personal teaching style. To the degree that it was possible, I believed in individualized instruction, in which my students learned the curriculum at their own, individual paces. I organized a very rich environment that contained a wide range of learning materials so that students were not restrained from learning concepts far above grade level. I created many learning centers that students could visit and explore throughout the day. I taught science, language arts, mathematics, art, and music using an integrated, interdisciplinary approach. To meet varying needs for direct instruction, I formed small groups to work with me on specific skills and to clarify concepts. I rarely taught the class as a whole group unless it was to introduce a brand-new, grade-level concept or for recreational activities such as singing, learning to play the flutophone (a small, plastic musical instrument), or playing games.

Walter was enchanted with this approach to teaching, and he frequently encouraged me by bringing visitors to my room and by photographing my work with children. He knew that I was a "seeker" and that, through my tendency to be an avid reader, I stayed on top of the latest educational research. Because of that, he trusted my professional judgment and gave me a lot of latitude. I'm grateful that he gave me the freedom to try new things,

Walter nominated me for the Who's Who Among America's Teachers Award. My name was published in the national publication in 1973. I always considered him a sponsor.

Walter Young is gone now, but he is not forgotten.

-Meltdown-

By this time, there were three school-aged children in our family. I hired Victoria Gonzales, a young woman from El Salvador, to be my fulltime, live-in housekeeper/babysitter. She made life easier for me by cleaning my house and babysitting my young children. This freed me to work later (as I had a tendency to do), attend night meetings, read more books, and spend more time with a handful of my friends. My ability to speak Spanish fluently enhanced our relationship, and Victoria was very loyal. I paid her fifty dollars a week from my salary. It was well worth it.

But the old adage, "All that glitters is not gold," could be aptly applied here. The children had few responsibilities for work around the house. They didn't learn early to share in chores, engage in teamwork to accomplish tasks, and genuinely support each other to the extent that I would have liked. I couldn't see it then, but this developmental lapse has played out well into their adulthood. It has been painful to observe my children's lack of cooperative ability at times, knowing full well that I inadvertently fostered it by not requiring more of them and by not monitoring as consistently as I should have their growth in the right direction. Poverty is not great, but affluence has its rotten fruit, too—it's called, *in*dependence, not *inter*dependence. I would have preferred the latter in my family. What I got is the price I paid for my own self-absorption.

I was sad and unfulfilled in my personal life. Marriage had been fraught with disappointment—for both Ken and me. I was unhappy, but I couldn't articulate the exact cause. I lived in a nice house; I had a nice car, plenty to eat, and beautiful children. Yet I felt isolated from what I wanted most—intimacy. I threw myself into my work and read dozens of self-help books trying to assuage the nagging emptiness that tugged at me. My sadness did not go unnoticed. People at work admonished me to take care of myself. Finally, I consulted a psychotherapist for help.

"Find someone who'll love you, Shirley," he said. "You're worth it." That was all he said as he handed me tissue after tissue to dry my seemingly endless flow of tears.

Marriage changes everybody. It changed me substantially. In spite of some domestic skills that I possessed, I was ill-prepared for the demands of cohabitation and marital commitment. To my advantage, I had never had a room to myself in my entire life. There was no bedroom, attic, or basement room ever designated *mine*—for just me and my things, so I didn't get paranoid about sharing space with my new spouse. But I lacked certain other qualities that were needed to transfer to marriage if, for my part, it was to have a chance for success. I knew little, for example, about building an intimate romantic relationship with a man. I had not seen this modeled in my home. I knew it was important, but I just didn't have a clue how to do it. Neither did I know how to stand up for myself in a relationship with a domineering partner. I had witnessed violence and wanted no part of it in my marriage, but I didn't know how to negotiate what I did want.

Ken, too, lacked important partnering qualities: he had poor verbal communication skills, vis-à-vis the ability to say what was on his mind, and knew virtually nothing about expressing deep emotional feelings, except those of disapproval. I was gregarious and outgoing; he, by contrast, was quiet and reserved. We struggled to reach mutual ground with shallow indicators of compatibility. We never really developed those higher levels of intimacy and trust that would predict a successful marriage.

Every year, out of frustration, I read every new self-help book that hit the market trying to understand the *why* of our awkward relationship: *Psycho-Cybernetics*[1]; *On Becoming a Person*[2]; *I'm OK, You're OK*[3]; and many, many more. I was convinced there was something

3   Maxwell Maltz, *Psycho-Cybernetics* (Englewood Cliffs, N J: Prentice-Hall, Inc. 1960).

4   Carl Rogers, *On Becoming a Person* (New York: Houghton-Mifflin, 1961).

5   Thomas A. Harris, *I'm OK, You're OK* (New York: Avon Books, 1967).

seriously wrong with me. I searched the psychology literature top to bottom trying to find it. There were times when I actually wanted to end my life.

It wasn't until many years after the marriage ended that I finally read something that registered as a plausible explanation. It was in a thick book called *The New Personality Self-Portrait: Why You Think, Work, Love, and Act the Way You Do* [4] that analyzed personality types. In it, I found descriptions of what I believe to have been my own and Ken's personalities as they were manifested at that time in our adult development. The book described and analyzed fourteen personality types. According to my understanding of the book, Ken had a personality that was a combination of "serious," "solitary," "leisurely," and "passive-aggressive." He enjoyed solitude. He could entertain himself with independent computer-related work and hands-on projects around the house for hours on end, or he could be happy just going fishing alone at a quiet lake and staying for a couple of days uninterrupted by anyone's demands. He not only enjoyed being alone, he preferred it to being around a lot of people, including me at times. I perceived this as his rejecting me, and it hurt.

He was reliable about paying the bills, and he worked hard at his job, but romance (with me) was not his strong suit. He preferred a good crossword puzzle to cuddling while listening to music beside a crackling fireplace, which was my idea of romance. When pushed too hard to exert more responsiveness or to participate in what he was not interested in, and when he felt irritated by some remark or behavior of mine, he could revert to passive-aggressive behavior. He would clam up and just withdraw...for days. In popular vernacular, I guess one might say that he just wasn't that "into" me; at least it seemed that way.

I, on the other hand, possessed elements of several of the different personalities that Oldham and Morris described. I've identified with the types they labeled as "sensitive," "conscientious," "self-sacrificing," "self-confident," and "mercurial." These combined personalities were well integrated in me, and I had "serious" and "passive-aggressive"

6   John M. Oldham, MD, and Lois B. Morris, *The New Personality Self-Portrait: Why You Think, Work, Love, and Act the Way You Do* (New York: Bantam Books, 1995).

personality traits, too. In short, I was a very complex individual! I loved being with other people and looked for opportunities to lead as well as support social activities. Additionally, I had a tendency to be quite self-sacrificing—always suppressing my own wants, wishes, and desires in order to fulfill the needs of others: friends, family, and the like. However, I also needed a lot of approval. On the surface, I projected self-confidence, but inside I was sensitive and could be deeply hurt by criticism (something I got a lot of from Ken). How much of my feelings were based on projections from my past, I don't know. It's possible, and even probable that I was hypersensitive to criticism because of what I had internalized from Mama's long, guilt-producing lectures when I was a child. All I know is that I didn't like it. I craved his attention, adoration, protection, and praise but did not know how to either get it or give it—not in the ways Ken might have wanted it (he sometimes mentioned "feminine wiles," of which I knew nothing).

Nonetheless, I was devoted to the marriage and truly tried to please him, to the sacrifice of some of my own core values, such as religion and church attendance. We never went to church together. I always wanted that. I conscientiously attended church well into my fifties, but after awhile, when they were young and resistant, I stopped taking the kids, and I didn't force them to go. I believe this was one of my greatest mistakes.

In the absence of a close marital relationship, I found my fulfillment in talking for hours on the phone with my friends and in the parenting of our children. Mothering also allowed me to sublimate the demands of an insensitive husband that made me feel inadequate. I got my love from the children. I busied myself with them and their demands. This was *my* passive-aggressive side at work.

I doted on the kids (my friends called me "super mom"), and I pretended that it was all right that I didn't feel the love and admiration that I longed for and had expected when I'd married. I feigned forbearance by projecting my self-confident, conscientious sides, but deep down I felt very lonely. I had wanted companionship, intimacy, and respect from marriage. I can't say for sure what Ken had wanted and expected (we never had those conversations), but I'm pretty sure it wasn't three kids and so much responsibility so soon.

In the early years of our marriage, no one picked up on this. To family and friends, we seemed to be the ideal couple. We put up a good facade that, at times, we even believed ourselves.

We both participated for a session or two in marital counseling, but Ken would not stick with it. I did, and I grew stronger. I learned to trust my own instincts and to express myself more assertively. My new demeanor caused Ken and me to become more distant. We were a train-wreck looking for a place to happen. Ken sought companionship (and compatibility) outside of our marriage with another woman. Fifteen and a half years into our marriage, the cars finally derailed. I was worn down by nearly nine years of living in an anemic, fragile marriage and by the knowledge (and sometimes visible evidence) that there was a third party involved. I was ready for a change.

"Irreconcilable differences" it would later be called in divorce court. That was a nice euphemism for "failure." It has been said that when failure occurs in interpersonal relationships, it is because somebody disappointed somebody. There was disappointment enough to go around between the two of us. But we hung on for a little while longer.

❦

-Out of the Classroom, into Politics-

Bob Farrell, a fellow UCLA student with whom I'd shared a few conversations on campus when we were in college there, became councilman of one of the largest districts in the city of Los Angeles: the Eighth District. He was appointed to fill the remaining term of Billy Mills, who had served a long term but had just received an appointment to the judicial bench. I remembered Bob as optimistic and altruistic.

Just where I got the nerve to call him and ask him for a job, I don't know. But I needed a radical change from where I was in my life. Frightening though it was, I was ready to leave the only profession I'd known, teaching, to try something different. I wanted what I did to be meaningful, but I really wanted it to be different. Also,

I hoped to earn more money. I was ready to move up and on from there. I had decided to leave my marriage, and I would need to be able to afford life on my own.

When I called Bob, he remembered me from school and was glad to hear from me again. After a lengthy phone conversation, in which we caught up on personal things, we made an appointment to talk in his Broadway Avenue field office. I expected our first encounter to be brief, but, instead, the meeting lasted three hours. We talked animatedly about the state of educational outcomes as measured by test results in the twenty-eight schools in his district. The scores were dismal and getting worse. Together, we connected the dots between educational standards, high school graduation rates, and the overwhelming conditions of crime and poverty that characterized the district's profile. Bob was passionate about doing something to bring about needed academic improvements and reverse the downward spiraling of the schools in his district. At stake were five failing high schools: Locke, Jordan, Fremont, Manual Arts, and Washington. Hundreds of young blacks and Hispanics were relying on these schools to prepare them for a better future—high-paying jobs and better homes and neighborhoods—but a failing school system was letting them down. It was time for action.

By the time the meeting was over, he offered me a consultant's position on his staff. There had never been an educational consultant assigned to a councilman's office; this would be a first. The pay was quasi-administrative—ten thousand dollars higher than I was earning on the twelve-year teacher's schedule that I was on. I was stoked!

On the way home, I rehearsed how I would break the news to Kenneth. I just knew he would disapprove. I was wrong. When I asked for his opinion, what he gave me was far more than I'd expected and far more than he had intended. We had not been speaking to each other for about two weeks—another of the episodes of silence that occurred regularly in our relationship. I approached him for an "appointment" to discuss something that I needed his opinion on. We agreed to meet in the children's bedroom at a specific time. We stood across the room from each other. I initiated the conversation by telling him of my meeting with Bob and the offer that was on the table. I sincerely valued Ken's opinion in matters like this one. He was very bright, and, with his analytical, mathematical mind, he could be very objective. Whatever he told me, I generally believed. This time, though, I was totally unprepared for his words.

"I think a guy like Bob Farrell would be damned lucky to get someone like you on his staff. You have a magnanimous personality, you meet no strangers, and you can relate from top to bottom of the social continuum with ease. And you speak Spanish well. That should be a great asset to him. If I were a guy going somewhere, like Bob, I definitely would want someone like you right by my side. When do you start?"

Just like that, my husband spoke the very first words of approval for me, as a person, that I had ever heard leave his lips. I was floored! Choking back tears, I thanked him. The meeting was over. I called Bob's office and set up my start date.

I can never express in words the significance of that day. It was simultaneously the beginning of a brand-new future and the end of an unsettled past. I had waited fifteen years to hear Ken's genuine thoughts about me; his words of praise and admiration, affirming words, meant a lot to me. But they came way too late. I already had one foot out the door. It was just a matter of time.

When Ken and I decided to get divorced, (or, more accurately, when I decided to get a divorce) everyone we knew was stunned, including our very own children. They hadn't seen it coming. Caryn and Ellen, who were eight and six years old, respectively, went with me, but Bruce, who was approaching twelve, elected to stay at home with his dad. Though it seemed okay at the time, this split in our family, leaving one sibling behind to feel abandoned, has resulted in an uncomfortable divide that to this day still seeks complete resolution. I've come to believe that Humpty Dumpty, once shattered, can never, truly, be put together again.

Meanwhile, my new job turned out to be very fulfilling. It was a one-hundred-eighty-degree change from teaching. The pace was brisk, and the activities were very stimulating. It was a time of enormous change in the city, of which the legendary Tom Bradley was the mayor.

Councilman Farrell had an ambitious vision for his district, which included high-performing schools. Together, we spearheaded several initiatives that were eventually implemented in the schools. One was the removal of junk foods from vending machines located on school campuses. Another was an introduction to the idea of creating magnet schools, which, according to our concept, would involve the creation of specialized schools-within-a-school, or SWAS as they would come to be called. This idea evolved from a visit to the famous Skyline magnet high school in Dallas, Texas, to which Bob sent me to gather facts about how the school had been conceptualized and how it was run.

Bob wanted to suggest that something like Skyline's educational approach, which focused on providing industrial and practical arts skills, become an offering for Eighth District pupils. The approach seemed not only relevant but prudent for our students, as an option to the college prep courses that they were failing in large numbers. It was one of the ideas that eventually caught on in the district. We couldn't be sure, however, whether it was because of us or just because there was a strong movement underway to change schools everywhere.

What we were sure of was that parents in the Eighth Councilmanic District became more involved in educational issues. We accomplished that by organizing existing, community-based, grassroots organizations, such as the Welfare Mothers, headed by a dynamic woman, Johnnie Blackmon, and other neighborhood entities such as churches, youth groups, and civic clubs. We met with them on a regular basis and kept them informed about issues affecting their children's schools. When it was important to "stack" the school board room with parents, we could do that by calling up our troops. Few critical decisions that involved schools in our district took place without the attention of Eighth District parents and active student groups.

In many ways, the work I did with Bob Farrell helped define me to myself. I found parts of myself that I didn't know existed. I did not do all of my work between the hours of nine and five. There were many times when I dressed up in long gowns and went out to glitzy banquets, cocktail parties, and various other evening events as a representative of the councilman. This was the glamorous side of the job. I had never seen myself this way in public before. Ken had been right; the role suited me perfectly. I especially enjoyed getting opportunities to introduce famous people to large audiences from time to time. Willie Brown, the renowned former speaker of the California House of Representatives, and Muhammad Ali were my favorites. Willie was so classy, and Muhammad Ali was just hilariously funny.

Once, when I was about to introduce him to an audience of middle school children, Ali and I waited backstage. He began kibitzing with me, saying funny things and asking silly questions.

"Is them your real teeth?" he asked me, pretending to inspect my teeth up close.

I responded in kind with my own question: "Yes, is them *yours?*"

He glared at me menacingly, the way he used to glare when he was trying to intimidate his boxing ring opponents. Then he turned away and walked onto the stage alone. It was so funny.

I truly enjoyed my work with Bob Farrell. It was never dull.

-Ernie Sprinkles-

Two weeks after I started my new job as councilmanic aide to Bob Farrell, I was called into his office to meet a new staffer. Bob introduced me to Ernest Sprinkles, his new deputy, who would be in charge of economic development in the district. Ernie was well known in the Southern California region. He had recently resigned from a very powerful position as executive director of one of the largest antipoverty programs in President Lyndon Johnson's administration, the Economic and Youth Opportunity Act (EYOA). His program budget was enormous for those days, and so was his salary. He was one of the highest-paid black persons west of the Rockies before he resigned his position amid political controversy. He earned a lot and spent a lot— partly out of tremendous generosity. He knew a lot of people. Many of them were big names among politicians and a good many of them were heavy-hitting power brokers. Generally, Ernie was a well-liked person. He had helped many people. Bob wanted his help now to get things going in his district.

I remember to this day the warm wave that swept over me as Ernie Sprinkles grinned, took my hand, and said, "Hello, pretty lady." There was something unforgettable in his charisma, his style, and his appearance. His salt and pepper Afro-styled hair was neatly coiffed. He was immaculately dressed; his colors were carefully coordinated, pressed, and matching. Physically, he was short, medium-built, and what the kids called buffed. I was immediately taken by him.

I could tell he liked me too—more than just a little. It's fair to say that we were magnetized to each other almost instantly. We exchanged friendly and funny banter before I left the office to resume my work. That was the first but not the last such encounter I would have with this charming man. The chemistry between us percolated to the surface right from the start. Any fool could see where we were headed.

I'm sure, now that I think back on the situation, that two people with strong "mercurial" personality traits met up in that office on that fateful day. Ernie had all of the dominant characteristics of this type of individual: he was outgoing, witty, charming, playful, and fun to be around. Typical of this type (according to Oldham and Morris), he quickly made up his mind and zeroed in on something he had been looking for that he found in me. Others in the office and around City Hall saw it long before I did.

I was placed in proximity to Ernie as we worked side by side on projects and rode back and forth in the same car to meetings and to the field office. Time together fostered a comfortable, warm, and fun friendship. I shared a lot with him about my home situation and confided that I was planning to leave. When I began searching the newspapers for apartments, he offered to help me select one that would be most suitable for me and the children. He thought I was very naïve about what I was opting into, and said he wanted to buffer some of that for me…as a friend—just a friend. I thought he was the most generous, caring man I'd ever met. No "suitable" place was ever found as a result of Ernie's search.

As a temporary solution, he proposed that the girls and I move into the graciously furnished, modern townhouse that he was leasing on Bundy Drive in Santa Monica. It was a very nice place—one that I would never have been able to afford on my own. We could utilize all the furnishings (dishes, utensils, pots and pans, included) until the end of the school year. Ernie would move his personal belongings and his clothes and live with a friend during the interim. We would split the rent for the townhouse fifty-fifty. What a deal! My problem was solved; I didn't have to move anything except our clothes and the girls' toys. And, the girls would attend the school with the best academic record in the school district to boot.

I felt funny about all this; frankly, it seemed too good to be true, but I was too grateful to care. It meant that I would not have to take anything from Bruce, who would be staying at home with his father. I didn't feel so guilty when I considered that, physically, if not emotionally, Bruce's home would remain in tact. Somehow, I thought that would make the changes less painful for him. I also thought that he would one day change his mind and come live with me and the girls.

Steady contact between Ernie and me and growing emotional attachment on both our parts eventually evolved into romance. Possessing the traits attributed to the mercurial personality, we were both prone to gravitate toward romance and strong emotional expression. The boundaries of that expression seemed limitless. Additionally, we shared deep philosophical convictions: about life and its meaning, about love and its power, about God, and on and on. My needs for attention, respect, and closeness were very well met in our relationship. Ernie was affectionate, attentive, and expressive. We talked about everything, sometimes for hours, and touched a lot. He called me several times a day from wherever he was. Sometimes he would show up unexpectedly at some meeting I was attending or return to the office to take me to lunch. Any excuse to be alone with me would do.

This new man in my life saw all manner of potential in me (that I had not seen in myself) and sought to bring it out (Mr. Mercurial in action): he bought me expensive designer clothes, paid to have my hair and nails done at exclusive salons, took me to nice restaurants, and otherwise wined and dined me—all in the effort to enhance my self-concept and shore up my weakened self-esteem. He thought I deserved the best. His pursuit was irrepressible and oh-so intoxicating. He listened intently to my conversation and soon analyzed just what I wanted; he seemed to know exactly what made me happy, and he provided it. I could not, just then, see the needy person who lived behind Ernie's veil. In retrospect, I realize that I was pretty needy myself.

When it was time to release the townhouse back to him at the end of the school year (in accordance with our agreement), I found a nearby place that I could now afford and made plans to move into it as soon as school was out for the summer. Ernie came unglued when I shared this information with him. I had miscalculated how tightly the web had become woven. We were happy. I just thought I should keep my end of the bargain. Ernie thought otherwise. He wondered if I had decided to go back home or if I had met someone else.

"Are you still shopping?" he asked.

The answers were "no," "no," and "no!"

Ernie had grown very attached and possessive of the arrangement we had. He was at the townhouse as much as he wanted to be, he was always around the girls and me, and he had brought into our lives his young daughter from a previous marriage, Lisa, who was near Caryn's age and with whom my girls had developed a fond, sisterly bond.

One Sunday morning, he came over dressed for church and tearfully asked me if I would marry him. He explained in stammering sentences that he was fearful that he would lose me. It was a thought that he said he just couldn't bear to conceive. We had been so happy during this past year. He just couldn't imagine living without me.

I initially had my doubts. I wasn't sure, for one thing, that my divorce was final. It wasn't, but Ernie did the research and found out that it would be by the time of our wedding in late November. I hugged him tightly, reassured him of my deep love for him (which was genuine), and said, "yes." He began to gleefully spread the news. Together, and with a few of his closest friends, we began to plan a simple but elegant wedding.

I notified my ex-husband and son and my former in-laws of the plans with formal wedding invitations. I didn't know how else to break news they would not want to hear.

Second Marriage

When I stepped into the chapel of Guidance Religious Science Church, where Ernie and I were married, in my long, flowing, chocolate brown, low-cut dress, the audience caught its breath. No one expected this picture! We had decided on chocolate brown, beige, and coral as our colors. I had found the dress of my dreams, the very one that I had seen myself wearing in my dreams, at a local department store. I spotted it on a rack that was being transported in the elevator to the formal wear floor that I had just left upstairs in despair because I hadn't found the right dress. And it was my exact size—a perfect ten. Without trying it on, I grabbed it off the rack and headed for the nearest cashier. The choice and fit could not have been more perfect.

My handsomely attired, well-coiffed brother, Carl, who, with his long, wavy hairdo and well-fitting tuxedo, looked like a young Barry White, escorted me down the aisle. There were beautiful flowers and long, white candles awaiting me at the altar. Our three girls, cutely-dressed, with pretty curls in their hair, were our flower girls. My friend of many years, June O'Kelley Armstrong (whom I knew from Tucson), stood with me as matron of honor this time around. I felt like a queen. Ernie was so proud; one could almost see his vest buttons bursting as he nervously awaited me at the altar. He had dyed his hair for the occasion. This caused quite a stir in the audience, whose loud, roaring laughter I could hear from the vestibule where I was waiting. Jam-packed with Ernie's old and loyal friends, coworkers, and high political types who knew him well, the sanctuary rocked with mirth, jocular comments, and laughter at the sight of this man who had just erased twenty years with a bottle of tint.

This mirthful atmosphere characterized the whole event. It was serious during the vows, but mostly light and fun otherwise. The music was contemporary and soulfully delivered, and it captured well our feelings of joy and deep love. Our chocolate brown wedding was a resounding success, one that people still bring up in conversations. It was memorable. In many ways, it set the tone for the high side of the future rollercoaster ride that characterized our life together as a couple.

We honeymooned in exotic seaside motels in Carmel and Monterey, California. We stopped all along the coast going and coming to take in the beauty of the ocean and the beautiful restaurants that darted the landscape. I had never experienced such a wonderful, romantic interlude with a man. This was the nature of my second husband. He lived every moment to the max. In his world, tomorrow would take care of itself; he lived for today.

During the course of our eight-year marriage, which would ultimately end in divorce, we Sprinkles accomplished a lot: we bought and furnished my dream house in the hills of Culver City, opened and operated a uniform vending business enterprise, traveled a little, and brought into the world a wonderful baby son, Jonathan. We had it all: love, romance, an affluent lifestyle, social prominence, and our own business.

By the time Ernie and I finally called it quits, we had succumbed to the pressures of over-ambitiousness. It was a classic case of fiscal imprudence in a horrible economic and financial climate (interest rates of fifteen and a half percent), plus the challenges of attempting to blend two very different families during the teen years. We were broke, and we had become disoriented from our goals as a couple. Our once tranquil vessel was tossing about in a sea of marital discord, like a ship without a rudder.

Ernie accused me of not knowing how to support a black man.

"You don't know what it's like to bust your butt out here, trying to make it in a white man's world," Ernie said to me one day. "You can't be scared to take risks. You have to have money to make money." Though there was some veracity in what he said, most of it was pure rhetoric. Rhetoric, rhetoric, rhetoric!

It was his rationale for taking out yet another mortgage on our home to finance his obviously failing uniform business. But the truth was, he was in a world about which he knew very little: sales. When

I started to work in the business he had set up, I found that he had hired five salesmen, whom he had gotten from the Urban League's job placement office. Each of them had been given a territory, a desk with a telephone, some catalogs, and a salary. These were not commissioned salespersons, they were drawing a salary. It wasn't long before I had fired every one of them. One was running his music business from our office, another was running up the phone bill by making long distance calls to a girlfriend in another state, and two never came in to work until noon. The only true salesperson was a Vietnamese woman who went out and brought in revenue from sales every day. No wonder we were going broke! I took charge of things, then and there.

By then, I certainly did know what it was like to "bust my butt." I was busting mine every day, driving all over LA County selling uniforms off of a thirty-foot minivan. Whatever money was made, I was making it the hard way—work! Every day I brought home between three and five hundred dollars. At one point, I even negotiated a contract with Rockwell International (the former U.S. defense company) to manufacture two hundred lab jackets and deliver them within two weeks. I was insane. I was also desperate. We needed the ten thousand dollars that I netted from the sale to keep the doors of our business open. I had expected to just place an order for the jackets from our supplier in Florida, but when I called, I was told that our account was deeply in the arrears and on its way to collections. They wouldn't ship me even *one* jacket. The only solution was to make them ourselves if I was going to keep good faith with our customer. I believed it could be done, and, although it nearly killed me, we it did.

There were other factors, but these were the salient ones, that caused the demise of our marriage. For me, the death knell was named trust. I lost it for Ernie, and, though he never said so, I suspect that, on some level, he lost it for me, as well. There was no other woman or man, just wild, reckless decision-making and exorbitant, ill-advised spending that eroded both our resources and the confidence that I once had in him. It was that confidence that I needed in order for me to feel safe. I had children to raise. I could be poor by myself; I didn't need a man to help me do that! The bubble finally burst, and Ernie and I walked away from each other, wounded but still friends.

-On My Own-

I had worked hard selling uniforms for the uniform company. Along the way, I'd developed a side business that involved actually manufacturing (designing and sewing) children's clothes. My Sprinkles of California clothing line consisted of sportswear for young girls. I turned my back on the uniform business and became immersed in efforts to make the new company succeed. I even entered trade shows and traveled with samples to places such as the Dallas Fashion Mart and attracted several out-of-state customers. The clothes were attractive but never sold in large enough volume to be profitable.

However, I did attract business from a few lucrative sewing accounts. The small, "quality" sewing shop, as it was called in the industry, received an order and sewed eight hundred theme dresses that were sold in Epcot Center stores when Disneyworld first opened. It continued to be a lucrative account for several months as we sewed the little dresses to stock the stores. We sewed, thereafter, for several high-fashion retail shops. The work was demanding. Good employees were expensive. My job, aside from sales, was to ensure quality. I pressed, cut thread ravels, and did the final inspections and bagging of garments.

Great friends, like Etha Robinson, a science teacher whom I'd met when she interned in our uniform shop to learn about business as a participant in a special community/business exchange that was sponsored by LAUSD and cooperating local businesses, sometimes voluntarily helped me. One night Etha and I ironed and bagged two hundred dresses to fill an order from the Army-Air Force Base Exchange. We worked all night in a local dry cleaners (the owner rented the space and equipment to me) that closed at 6:00 p.m. By the time they reopened at 6:00 a.m., we were done—and thoroughly exhausted!

I'll never forget my dear friend, Elgin "Tiger" Turner, a local black fabric cutter, who worked all night for two days helping me to get two hundred lab jackets for our customer, Rockwell International, correctly graded and cut out. Moreover, Tiger often loaned me large sums of money to meet my payroll. He also filled my freezer with meat when he knew I was low on grocery money for my family.

(As the eldest of twelve siblings, Tiger understood what it was like to need things that one could not afford to buy. How many times had he personally experienced that situation in his own life?) He brought the meat over to our house on the pretext that his home's freezer would not hold any more, so he needed to "store" it in mine. His was certainly the helping hand that often made a difference in my life. He, like many people, was pulling for my success. Some pulled harder than others.

Regrettably, I was unable to sustain the sewing business while warding off financial and marital shipwreck at home. Ultimately, to keep from sinking too far, I closed the doors of the business and went home to think. I was heartbroken and stubborn. I'd poured so much into making my business work.

On a gloomy, overcast day, much like the day I see out my a window as I write this account, I sat alone on the white, Haitian, cotton sectional sofa that had so elegantly graced my living room for the past five years. It had been the special gift of a doting new husband, who, at that time, wanted me to have anything I could dream of. Observing the soil imposed on the multi-cushioned circular couch by both time and four growing children, I smiled the wry smile of metacognition—the frivolity of such an impractical purchase finally settled in. What had I been thinking? What could I have expected? A white sofa made absolutely no sense. Making sense was not my strong suit at age thirty-seven. The obvious inappropriateness of a white sofa for a family like mine was only one of several realities I was facing on that gloomy day. The most weighted one was the imminent loss of my treasured home in the foothills of a prestigious Culver City neighborhood. I had had my day in foreclosure court and lost. I was being evicted. *I*, "Miss Most Likely to Succeed," was being evicted!

Although I was out of time, I couldn't control my ego. In spite of every prevailing fact that I could clearly see, I insisted on overriding the urgings of my rational mind, which told me to just face the reality and start packing. Instead of spending my limited time packing up my crap and getting ready to move, I was thinking up new "rabbit trails" to pursue in hopes of avoiding the inevitable.

It was at the end of the last trail that I picked up the phone and called my mother. This was, truly, my last chance. I would not have wanted to do this if there were even a teeny-weeny alternative available to me. My defeat—any form of failure—was not something I ever wanted exposed to Mama.

My mother had been fond of Kenneth, my first husband; he was the mathematician with a brain that she admired. She had been less fond of my second husband, who she perceived to be a schemer. Therefore, when trouble had arisen in marriage number two, she had not been very sympathetic. She had stood back and just watched the dominoes fall. Now it was the house that was tumbling. How, oh how, I hated to make that call!

"Hi, Mom," I said when she answered the phone. "I'm calling to ask a big favor."

"Okay," she replied. "What?"

"I was wondering what you think about buying my house? It's probably the only way I can save it from foreclosure. Are you willing to do that?"

There was a long silence on the other end of the line.

"Mom, are you there?" I could hear myself sounding pitiful, but I couldn't help it.

"Yeah, I'm here," she said. "I'm thinking."

Another long pause took place. I began filling the silence with chatter, explaining what would be needed. "There's a fifty thousand dollar balloon payment due January 1, and I don't have the money. If you could just pay that off for me, it would give you a trust deed on the house, and I could pay you back the money. I can afford the notes on the first and second mortgages, but I've been paying seven hundred fifty dollars a month on this damned third—interest only. I can barely keep my head above water. I'm behind in all the utilities, but I do pay something every month just to keep them on."

I took a deep breath and was about to start a new sentence when Mama blurted out, "How the hell did you get yourself into this fix? Three trust deeds on that house? Y'all must have been thinking with your behinds, 'cause you sure weren't thinking with your heads. You didn't pay but fifty-four thousand dollars for that house! How could you have tied it up like this?"

I struggled to explain how we had borrowed to support the uniform vending business that my husband had started. "Mama, I only began paying attention to what was happening with the borrowed money when I started working in the business myself. I was in la-la land, I guess. I signed anything he put before me."

Ernie had a way of sweet-talking that made me feel special. I'd have trusted him to the moon and back. In fact, he made it sound as if he really wanted a piece of the moon, just for me. That man could "rap." Even after the myopia cleared up, and I could see what was going on, I still let him talk me into signing loan documents that were sheer treachery.

That was my story. Mama listened, but she didn't soften one whit. Ernie still owed her five thousand dollars that he had borrowed from her without telling me, and, five years later, she had not collected one dime of repayment. One day, after all the dust had settled, she would show me the promissory note he had given her.

"Well, the answer to your question is *no*," she finally said.

She knew about the small clothing manufacturing business that I had established and that I worked at keeping the business going every day (and night). She was only lukewarm about this enterprise. From her perspective, it kept us going all right, but there wasn't enough profit in it to do much more than keep us at the survival level.

I was pretty high on the business. I loved the challenge of being an entrepreneur, calling my own shots, and building clientele for my services and goods. It was intoxicating. A large part of me wanted to just hang on. My luck would change. I knew it would! And, wasn't everyone telling me to "hang in there"? I had tried everything to keep the doors open—even going on network television as a contestant on three game shows—*High Rollers, Press Your Luck*, and *Battlestars*—but my winnings had not covered my debts.

There had been other complications that injured the success of my business as well. One had dealt me a crushing blow. One day, I'd returned to the shop to find that all of the clothing we had just finished for my best-paying designer was gone. It was the middle of the day, and all of my sewers were gone too. The door was open, but they, and the garments I was waiting to get paid for, were all gone! Nothing was left except silent, barren sewing machines and other equipment we used in the shop. The black woman I had placed in charge during my absence had made a deal with the customer to set up the same operation in back of her store in Beverly Hills. She'd stabbed me in the back, so to speak, and taken all of my people with her—not to mention my money. Stunned and hurt beyond words, I had sat down and cried. It was my first lesson in "cutthroat" business ethics, and I hadn't seen how I would ever recover from it. I was paying dearly for lessons I never intended to learn.

What my mother could see that I couldn't was the high cost of absenteeism from my principal role in life—that of mothering and guiding my young children. Encouraging words were not paying the bills. She was not at all high on the business I had so much pride in. Her answer had a solid ring of finality: "No!"

I knew my chances of winning her over to my side were hanging by a very thin thread. Intuitively, I knew she had reasoned to herself during the silence: *She's drowning, and the fool can't see it. She's over her head in this water. Yeah, I could pull her to shore today if I wanted to. She knows I've got the money. But at the rate she's going, she still won't be able to climb out of the damned river!*

How many times had I heard Mama's admonition to "live within your means"? Well, I hadn't done that, and she was sorely disappointed in me. No was no—period. Now, as I hung up the phone to face the reality I dreaded, I knew I had to move out and move on.

Live within my means? What *means*? I had not one dime! I had used everything I had to stay put in that house. With no money for first, last, and security deposits on an apartment that came anywhere near what I would consider adequate, I had no other choice but to accept the one offer of help that Mama had presented: move back home and live above her in her upstairs duplex in South Central LA—yes, "the hood." The rent would be two hundred twenty-five dollars per month, due on the first.

I could have cried. Maybe I did—a little. Going back home was what other people did, not me! But, that's what I had to do. After I got over my pity party, my next call was to Jimmy Smith, another of my lifelong Tucson friends, who loved me dearly and would do anything to help me. I asked for his help to move my stuff to my mother's place. He said yes and asked no questions. He knew my situation and seemed relieved that I was making this step. We set a date. It was a done deal.

Facing my reality forced me to hear, and finally acknowledge, the truth of my mother's words about my business: I had a "no-business business." By that, she meant that I was busy enough, but that I was not making enough to pay myself. Therefore, I was in business for others, not myself.

The indisputable truth of her words caused me to reflect on what I had been "called" to do with my life. My calling was not to be a hardcore business woman. Yes, I loved the high I got when I proclaimed to others, "I own my own business!" And it was a kick to call my own shots on a daily basis. Entrepreneurship was totally intoxicating to this black woman. But I knew deep inside that I was born to teach. Teaching was as natural to me as flying was to a bird. Teaching had always been my true passion. Yet, somehow, it felt like failure to return to it after ten years of pursuing the exotic things I had been involved in. But I was broke. I needed money now, and I didn't know where to turn. With my world unraveling at a rapid pace, I had to have help to get through this period of uncertainty.

That's how I wound up in the welfare line in a north Hollywood social services office. Four-year-old Jonathan and I sat side by side in the folding metal seats that filled the large waiting room. Not a chair was vacant. There were a lot of people waiting to be interviewed for public assistance. The line seemed to go all the way out the door. After about two hours of shuffling down seat by seat, we finally were escorted into the glass-enclosed office of a weary intake consultant. As I turned to adjust my seat, I caught a glimpse through the window of the sea of waiting applicants. Something in that very instant, I don't know what, gripped my consciousness and shook it—hard!

There were some really traumatized and desperate people out there in that room. Their eyes seemed glazed over with pain and despair. I was not one of those. True, I was broke, financially, but I was not, by any definition, a welfare case. I was, in fact, very rich in other ways: I had a good education, I had marketable skills, I was good-looking, I was charming, and I even spoke fluent Spanish. I could work. Had I not learned self-reliance at my mother's knee? At minimum, I could return to my chosen profession, to my authentic vocation—I could teach.

It was a pivotal moment. I abruptly got up out of the chair I had sat down in. Without giving any explanation, I thanked the confused intake person, grabbed little Jonathan by the hand, and walked out. With determined steps, I headed straight for the administrative offices of the Los Angeles Unified School District to pick up where I'd left off ten years ago.

"Going home," in this instance, was not just moving upstairs over Mama's place; it was more like the return of a prodigal daughter to the place where she belonged.

Regrouping

-Sylvia Perea-

Sylvia Perea hired me to teach a bilingual kindergarten class at Trinity Street School in South Central Los Angeles. She was the dynamic, vivacious, principal of the large inner-city elementary school. I had never taught kindergarten, but I could speak Spanish fairly fluently. It was this skill that got me hired; otherwise, I would not have been qualified for any teaching position in the Los Angeles Unified School District at that time. Spanish-speaking teachers were in high demand. How grateful I was for my early exposure to the language and for the High Intensity Language Acquisition (HILA) courses that Walter Young had encouraged me to take.

After a short time in the classroom, Sylvia called me into her office to ask if I would be interested in entering a program to be trained for an administrative position. She said she saw leadership potential in me and encouraged me to let her recommend me for the two-year school district and Cal State University cooperative program. If I stayed with it and was successful, I would acquire both a master's degree and an administrative credential. I could soon become a vice principal and one day become a principal; thereby, I would get myself into a much higher pay structure within a short period of time.

It took me two seconds to say, "Sure! I'll do it!"

Two years later, I had that master's degree.

I will always be thankful to Sylvia Perea for sponsoring me onto the most important professional path of my lifetime. Not only did she save *my* life, in addition she laid the groundwork for my family's future, which was much improved by advancement in my professional career. The academic work was exhausting since I had to do it at the conclusion of fulltime teaching days and (in the second semester) an internship that challenged me to the gills. But it was all worth it; I'd do it all over again in a heartbeat.

I also learned to live within my means: I bought scaled down, secondhand furniture at consignment stores to furnish my tiny apartment; I sewed my own professional-looking clothing from piece-goods left over from my sewing business; and I cooked homemade foods like stews, casseroles, and beans. There were leftovers that lasted for days. Significantly, I also opened a savings account and learned to save something in it every month from the little check that was delivered in the mail.

In the eight years that followed the big move to Mama's house, good things happened: I cleaned up the bad credit left over from my second marriage and finally got on good, solid, financial ground; the children grew up; and the three older ones went to college. Two of them finished and landed fantastic jobs. I too moved up the ladder to more responsibility and higher pay. Doors of opportunity kept opening for me. Better prepared than ever, I walked through them.

Looking back, I'm proud of all of those accomplishments, but I'm also humbled and grateful that I was given the will, by a higher power, to keep going in the face of difficulties. Though there were many challenges and untold obstacles along my path, once I decided to resume teaching children, giving up never really crossed my mind. I'm so glad today that I didn't quit, because just around the corner was a destiny that I could not have imagined at the time.

-Bernie Goldstein-

Bernie Goldstein was the principal of Manchester Avenue School. He was a tall, heavyset, jovial, midfortyish Jewish man, whose hometown just happened to be Tucson, Arizona. He became my boss after I nearly destroyed my career in another school under a different principal. I had been pulled out of my kindergarten classroom to help a new black principal who was struggling with a variety of problems— not the least of which was that he didn't know what he was doing. My job, in essence, was to work in a quasi-administrative position, coordinating programs funded with state and federal monies.

It turned out to be much more than that. I was, in actuality, the functional vice principal of the school *and* the coordinator of special programs—both very demanding jobs. I loved the work, and the staff and children loved me, but the principal did not. After a very contentious semester, we needed to part ways if I was to keep my career from ending up in a ditch. I dressed in suits that had been given to me by a kind and generous Jewish fabric dealer who I did business with when I had my shop. They were very nice clothes, samples, that he had hanging around his store. I wore them with heels and accessorized them with simple jewelry. I just wanted to look professional and do my job well, but the principal perceived me to be threatening and ambitious for his job. I perceived him to be just plain incompetent. It was my move. I had to go.

At the request of the area superintendent, who seemed to realize that a serious mismatch had taken place in the assignment, Bernie Goldstein agreed to give me a chance to succeed on his campus. This time, it was a perfect match. In short, my tenure under his administration and leadership was a dream. It became a professional love affair. Once we got a couple of basic things straight up front, it was smooth sailing.

Bernie's first words to me were: "Shirley, remember *I'm* the principal here!"

No other words were needed. I understood the message and was more than glad to let him do his job so I could do mine: that of coordinating specially funded educational programs for bilingual, gifted, and other special needs children, such as those needing compensatory education (Title I). Bernie Goldstein came to trust me for what I could do. I knew my area of work well. I never let him down. I will never forget the professional confidence this relationship instilled in me. Bernie was tough, bright, and confident. So was I, and I measured up.

Moving On and Moving Up

-Linda Wisher-

Linda Wisher was assistant superintendent of the Moreno Valley Unified School District when she came to Bernie's school, Manchester Avenue Elementary, to interview me for a district-level job. The position was assistant coordinator of state and federal programs—it would pay twenty-five thousand dollars, more than I was currently making.

To make a long story short, by the time Linda left, I was the new hire. I was ecstatic. I was sad to leave Bernie and our staff and students, but it was an opportunity I could only have dreamed of. It meant moving ninety miles east of Los Angeles to a new city, but I was ready for the change it would bring in my life.

When the time came, I enthusiastically made the move. Initially, I rented a room from a widowed black lady in the Moreno Valley community. By the time I learned that she wanted to retire and move to Florida, I was financially able to make an offer on the lovely, three-bedroom, cottage-styled home I lived in. It was a God-given favor that I received with thanksgiving another opportunity to have something I treasured that had been lost: my own home.

The family had scattered to far-flung places: Caryn, who now had a child of her own, was living in San Diego; Bruce was out of college, working, and living independently in Orange County; Ellen was attending Journalism School at the University of Colorado at Boulder; and Jonathan had long been living with his father, Ernie, in Oxnard, California. I was free to move up the ladder, unencumbered by dependent children.

For a time, things went well. There was much to do, especially in the Bilingual Program that had been long neglected and was now under scrutiny by the California State Department of Education. This work was just up my alley. I plunged in up to my neck.

Linda Wisher talked to me at length during our first official meeting. She was sincere about improving the learning and teaching situation for Limited English Proficient (LEP) students in her district. I was sure I knew what she wanted me to do. I was eager to get started fixing things. I would work closely with the district's coordinator of special programs, Marti Ord.

One night, a "call" meeting took place; the meeting had been called by a group of local parents of LEP students—mostly, if not all, Hispanic. Marti knew about the meeting, but she did not attend. We expected about two dozen parents; instead, more than one hundred showed up!

They were polite but vocal about their demands for improvement: more teachers, more materials, more parental involvement, etc. I had been asked to sit on the end of the small panel of district officials who were to answer questions and present information. I was new and black, not Hispanic. I was not given a role to play other than my presence as a representative of our department. The atmosphere grew tenser and tenser as the meeting droned on, dominated by district personnel making "presentations." Hardly anyone seemed to be actively listening, but the audience of parents was, nevertheless, polite.

Then, one of the parents, a well-educated Hispanic father, raised his hand and commenced to speak in Spanish. He asked the other parents in attendance to address their remarks to the panel in their native language as well. He said, "I'm not interested in the cute pie charts and fancy graphs that have been presented here tonight. I and these other parents want to know—what is going to be done about the mess the district is in regarding our children's education?"

The room fell silent, waiting for the staff's response. Faces on the panel turned every shade of red imaginable. None of the highly paid administrators had understood a word of the question. They looked at each other in bewilderment. Finally, Linda peered down the long table where the panel sat, leaned forward toward me, and asked if I understood what had been said. Of course, I did. I possessed a Bilingual Certificate of Competence that I had earned from the state of California! I could speak, read, and write Spanish very fluently—a fact that hadn't mattered until now. Earlier in the day, when we were planning for the meeting, my opinions had either not been requested, or they had been dismissed as irrelevant. It was my time to shine.

After interpreting the question for my colleagues, I proceeded to take over the meeting, responding in Spanish to one question after another. I told the parents, "I've been hired by the district to address the problems you've brought forth. We are aware of these problems, and I fully intend to work with the administration to bring about resolution to as many as possible, but you must be our helpers. We will need your help and guidance along the way."

I solicited parent volunteers to serve on a bilingual parent advisory council. I had learned to handle this type of situation while working in Bob Farrell's political arena. I was comfortable with controversy, and I knew just how to redirect an angry crowd.

Bob had once called in the TV news media and, before rolling cameras, threatened to close down Manual Arts High School if parents did not show more interest in the school. This was following the first shooting murder of a student in broad daylight on the campus during school hours. He had been angry because no parents had shown up, and most of the students and teachers had gone home by the time he and I had arrived just after lunchtime. An angry crowd had come to the meeting he called in the school's auditorium that evening. Helicopters had circled in the air over the campus, and armed policemen had patrolled the surrounding streets. After much heated debate about the pros and cons of his proposal, he had calmed the crowd down by calling for a problem-solving task force that they could sign up for.

I employed that tactic here with good results. As the sign-up sheet circulated, the atmosphere changed from one of hostility to one that was more conciliatory and calm. Everyone on the panel felt relief and was pleased to see how eager parents were to become involved.

Linda patted me on the back afterward and said, "Shirley, that was a masterful job!"

Unfortunately, Linda was forced to take an extended leave of absence due to her need to care for her critically-ill and elderly mother. That threw me into the "lion's den" with a new supervisor whose leadership style, educational philosophy, and personality clashed with mine. She was a product of what blacks called "white and right" Orange County. In Orange County, for the most part, there was scant sympathy for the plight of non-English speaking people. I, on the other hand, was fresh out of the sprawling, urban Los Angeles Unified School District environment, with *all* of its diversity; over one hundred and ten different languages were served in classrooms there every day, and every attempt was made to follow the letter as well as the spirit of the law. As a result of my professional indoctrination along those lines, I believed wholeheartedly in full implementation of bilingual education.

There were several thousand LEP students enrolled in my new district, with more coming in every day. Languages ranged from Spanish to Hmong, with several others, like Farsi, Vietnamese, and Armenian, in between. Virtually nothing had been done to address these students' needs. There had been no acknowledgment of the cultures represented by such a diverse group of students; there were Latinos, Chinese, Vietnamese, Iranians, and Armenians. No one in authority seemed to recognize the relationship of language to learning. Laws were in place to ensure that these students did not get lost along the way, academically.

I was on fire to bring about change for those students. Marti Ord resigned her position, and I was left to go it alone.

I developed an aggressive, focused staff development program for all staff—regular education teachers, bilingual education teachers, and administrators alike—so that everyone had the same information. I believed that we all needed to be on the same page in order to get things in proper order. I conducted training sessions on implementing specially designed instructional lessons for students whose languages we could not accommodate with a native-speaking teacher, and I ordered tons of instructional materials and brand-new Spanish language textbooks to address the needs of our largest population of LEP students.

My pace was not exactly aligned with that of my new supervisor—I was moving too fast for her. She dragged her feet about approving my purchase orders and my many requests for substitute teachers that were necessary to cover classes so that the bilingual staff could partake of sorely needed training. But the pace *was* aligned with the parents of those students and with the few bilingual teachers who had been struggling to implement the mandates of the state and federal laws.

My supervisor, Gena*, and I clashed almost daily over something. Memos flew back and forth. One day, she called me into her office. She shook her finger in my face and told me, "You *will* do what I tell you to do!"

"The last person who shook her finger in my face was my mama," I responded. "You sure don't look like Mama, so I'd advise you, respectfully, not to do that again."

"I'm fifty-two years old," I added, "and nobody, and I do mean *nobody*, shakes their finger in my face!"

I turned on my heels and left her office to cool off. It was one of many highly charged encounters between the two of us.

She frequently said I was "shooting myself in the foot."

I guess that was the cause of the pain I felt every day. The year was 1989, and I had read Dr. Wayne Dyer's book, *Pulling Your Own Strings*[1], about three times. I'd learned how to handle myself with overbearing people in the workplace.

Knowing what I know now, however, I'd probably treat that situation differently. I had a lot more to learn about bureaucracies and how they function at top levels. It was different down below at the classroom level. Not even mid-management effectively prepared me for the power struggles that routinely went on between coworkers in administration. It was a tension-filled environment much of the time. I would have more lessons and opportunities to learn them in the future.

Gena and I were two bright women who saw the world through very different filters. Our experiences, training, and expectations were worlds apart. We had lived and worked in two different paradigms. We just couldn't bridge the gap. My dignity was on the line…but so was hers. I had to go. Soon the hands of fate would conspire to send me off to take my chances in a new land—with a new job and a new love to boot.

1   Wayne Dyer, *Pulling Your Own Strings* (New York: Harper Collins, 1978).

Part V

Making Texas My Home...Again

The important thing is this: to be able at any moment to exchange what we are, for what we can become.

—Charles Duval

Fools' Gold

-Jay Once More-

March Air Force Base was in Riverside County, where I worked. One night I went to dinner on the base with Rosetta, my Tucson friend, and her husband, John Bullock. She worked in the school district I was now employed with (in fact, it was she who had told me about the opening in the first place), and he was a retired airman. A kind of déjà vu experience overcame me. I remembered Waco and began reminiscing about my old friend Jay, who had briefly been my fiancé. I wondered out loud about his whereabouts. I assumed that he was still in the air force, someplace in the world—probably happily married with a bunch of kids. With the help of a military acquaintance of Rosetta's, we located him. He was living in Austin, Texas. I even had an address. Temptation was too great to resist.

On a whim, I wrote him a playful letter, giving clues and hints as to my identity, but not enclosing a signature; he was to guess who I was from my clues. I gave my office number where he could reach me if he figured out who I was and wished to contact me for a friendly chat. Jay responded by telephoning me within minutes of opening my letter. He said he recognized my handwriting on the envelope and didn't need any further clues. He was delighted to hear from me, and now he wanted to see me. I wasn't sure how this could take place since we were far apart, and I didn't yet have a home to invite him to visit. We agreed to meet in Las Vegas one weekend soon to see each other again and catch up on things.

Our reunion in Vegas was exciting and fun. He looked thinner than I remembered, and he was older. Also, he was retired from the military after achieving the status of "Bird" colonel of a large base in

163

the Midwest, divorced, and raising a very young daughter from his second marriage.

This meeting started a rendezvous with destiny, the nature of which neither of us could have imagined. We both returned to our respective homes to resume our lives, but we had gotten reconnected, and now a new world was unfolding: two single and lonely people who mutually admired each other hooked up. After many hours of talking long distance, wired flowers and perfume, and a couple of trips between Texas and California, Jay once again proposed marriage. During our exchanges, he'd heard all about my troubles with Gena, and was very sympathetic and supportive.

This time, I was not so wary as before. I wanted out of Moreno Valley. Maybe this time marriage would work. I was ready to buy that "fried ice cream"!

Fortuitously, I had received a letter of solicitation and an application for a full scholarship to attend the University of Texas. It was from the Department of Bilingual Special Education, and it was specifically recruiting minority candidates for the doctoral degree. The application had sat on my desk for a couple of months. I looked at it often, thinking how many times I had dreamed of getting a doctorate; I had even written it into my long-range plans. But attaining the coveted terminal degree in expensive California schools seemed improbable, if not impossible. I was still recovering. I didn't have that kind of money.

Now, however, the opportunity to reach my highest goal began to seem more plausible. With Jay returning to the picture, I could leave the job that was rapidly making me sick, get married again to a really nice guy I at least *liked* a lot, move where he was, *and* pursue my doctorate degree.

When I left California, I left behind everything that I had accumulated materially and otherwise: my home, furnishings, family, and friends—everything. It was scary, but I was determined to give it a shot. I could not have imagined then how right that move would become for me. It was a leap of faith that paid off in spades.

Although I had lived quite successfully as a divorcée, making my own way in the world for eight years, I still longed for a solid love—yet another chance at marriage, a home, and happiness with a husband.

I was fifty-two years old, and alone was not where I'd planned to be. I moved to Texas with the anticipation of filling the void in my life. I had reconnected with an old suitor from Tucson days. We thought we could recapture something that was long gone.

We boldly plodded through our lurking doubts, ignoring little warning signs that I'm sure we both felt. Because we expected to one day blend our families, we lovebirds began right away looking for a large enough home to buy. After a couple of months, when we were unable to find what we thought we wanted, we contracted with a well-respected builder and commenced construction on a fabulous, four-bedroom, Spanish stucco house on a high hill in one of the most prestigious sections of Austin: Great Hills. It was thirty-six hundred square feet of luxury spread out over three levels and facing a magnificent view of the city. There were Saltillo-tiled floors throughout the lower level, a massive family room with a fireplace and many windows on the second level, four cozy bedrooms, and three and a half baths distributed between the first and third floors. A wide wooden deck was suspended over the hillside in the rear of the house that connected to the kitchen, living room, where there was another fireplace, and the master bedroom. From it, steps led downstairs to an outdoor terrace that featured a fifteen-by-thirteen-foot swimming pool located right on the cliff. It was a magnificent home, situated in the best location in town.

I supervised the whole project for Jay. He gave me a free hand in selecting all of the amenities: tiles, cabinets, hardware, countertops, paint colors, and carpets. To get the work done on schedule, I worked in meetings with designers and the contractors between my classes. I learned a lot and loved the fact that Jay trusted my judgment enough to give me carte blanche to design the home that he was investing so much into.

Once we moved in, or should I say *by the time* we moved in, it was eight months into the relationship, and things were not the same. There was trouble in the camp spelled, "e-x-w-i-f-e." Before I knew it, she was decorating my new house while I was away at classes at UT! And what's more, she did it with his permission and his money. What part of *stupid* did I not understand?

When I came to myself, I realized that Jay and I had unwittingly become a part in a silly and dangerous game. His ex-wife had walked away, but she'd kept one foot (and many of her personal possessions) in the door. He had always wanted her back. I was just a pawn in the whole ploy—an attractive lure. A young daughter, her only child and his youngest of four, was a key factor in the picture. They were both guiltily torn about her plight. She loved them both, but he had custody. It was an awkward arrangement. The triangle became uncomfortable for all involved. I should have known better; one should look before leaping. Luckily, I had taken the chance of applying for the UT scholarship before leaving Moreno Valley. To my delight, I was awarded the full scholarship in the fall of 1989, and had started taking graduate classes toward my PhD at the university when these domestic issues surfaced, so I just closed my eyes to the situation and immersed myself in my studies.

My son, Jonathan, then fourteen years old, had come to live with us. His father, who was ailing from lung cancer and was too sick to take care of him any longer, had sent him to Texas abruptly over the Christmas holidays. The kids did not get along well with each other. Jay's daughter was spoiled rotten, and so was Jonathan. Neither of them had had to share very much with anyone else. A silent war took place on a daily basis, with tattling going back and forth to her Mommy *and* to his Daddy. As for Jay, he began acting as if the wrong family had moved into the new house. Something fishy was going on. I was unable to detect just what it was. Soon there was misery all around. The tug on our relationship was overwhelming and suffocating at times. No one was really happy.

Ernie was dying of cancer back in California. He and Jonathan had a deep bond that had been interrupted by the illness. Jon couldn't wait to get back home with his dad again. He was packed up two weeks before he was to leave. He had a one-way ticket. Unfortunately, the night before he was to leave, Ernie called to tell me not to send Jonathan home. He said he was not in a position to take care of him yet. The news was so devastating to Jon that he closed his bedroom door and slammed his fist through one of the walls of his room.

A big hole was punched in a wall of Jay's precious new house! Sheepishly, Jon came downstairs to confess to me what he had done. Frustration had taken its toll on him. Fortunately, Jay was out of town until the next day. I was frantic. What would I tell him? How would I protect Jon from what I anticipated would be his certain anger?

All I could think of was how to get that wall repaired before Jay could see it that way. I knew more construction was taking place in the neighborhood, so I flew out of the house. Luckily, I did find a couple of workers finishing up for the day. I begged them in Spanish to follow me home and fix the wall. They did, and the wall was repaired as well as possible, though not perfectly. The plaster was still wet when I took Jay upstairs to see the damage. He was not a happy camper, but he kept his cool.

I sent Jonathan home to LA on his scheduled flight, but he stayed with my oldest daughter, Caryn, not with his dad. By now, you could cut the tension in the air of our house with a knife. Three days after Jon left, Jay and I had a huge fight that lasted all night. I told him what I thought of him—how arrogant, insensitive, and deceptive he was. He was angered by my remarks and threatened to put all my clothes and belongings out on the front lawn. When the fussing and cussing was over, we settled down, laughed heartily about the fight, and then we made passionate love. But it was too late. The kindling fire of that brief passion soon went cold again. He moved in with his ex a few days later, leaving me alone in the house.

She proceeded to completely redecorate our home. Every day when I got home, something new had been done. One day while I was at school, she completely redecorated our master bedroom: new curtains; bedspread; pillows; and covers for the round, glass-top bedside tables.

By now I had a full year of graduate work under my belt and a belly full of these shenanigans. I packed my belongings and moved out. My feelings ran the gamut: I was very hurt; I had no money, so I was scared; I was very angry; and, most of all, I felt very embarrassed. I gathered up my few belongings and, with the help of my college colleague and friend, James Hammond, I moved out.

Jonathan returned to Texas in time for the fall school semester. He could see that life with his father was not going to be possible,

although it broke his heart to acknowledge how sick his beloved
father and pal was. Nevertheless, they had spent some good, quality
time together while he was in California. I will always be glad that I
sent him. It was the last time he would see his father alive.

By then, I was settled into a comfortable, two-bedroom, modern
apartment a good distance from the house I'd helped to build, but
close enough, in terms of school boundaries, that Jon could continue
to go to school with his friends. To Jay's credit, my ex-fiancé paid the
initial costs of my relocation—first, last, and security fees—which
amounted to nearly three thousand dollars. It was the least he could
do, I thought. I secured employment with UT-Austin and vigorously
pursued my studies until I graduated three years later with a PhD in
educational administration. Because of the program I was in, I was
now qualified to be a school district superintendent—a job I would
never pursue because I could not leave Austin while my child was
still in school. He needed that kind of stability after what he had just
gone through. And women superintendents were the hardest to place
in Texas, especially black ones. This time I'd have to stand at the door
of opportunity and wait. Circumstances would not allow me to walk
in.

Jay's ex-wife never did move into the house on the hill. After I
was out of the picture, the two of them decided that they couldn't
put Humpty Dumpty together again, either. Sadly, a few years later,
she became ill and ultimately died. The loss to her young daughter
was immense.

Occasionally, Jay and I have run into each other in a restaurant
or at the neighborhood grocery store. Although we are amicable and
always genuinely glad to see each other (as old friends) during these
encounters, it will always feel awkward.

Higher Pursuits

-Nolan Estes-

There is no one in this world quite like Dr. Nolan Estes. He is in a class of his own, as far as I am concerned. He is super tall (about six feet six or seven), super magnanimous, and super generous. Dr. Estes was a nationally renowned educational leader. He had been the superintendent who had guided the Dallas Independent School District through several tumultuous years of school desegregation and had served in Washington DC as one of Lyndon B. Johnson's undersecretaries of education. For some reason, he saw to it that I was inducted into UT's Cooperative Superintendency Program (CSP) of which he was director. Only fifteen people out of over three hundred applicants would be accepted, and most were currently holding positions as principals or vice principals of Texas schools. The idea was to recruit and train the best new potential superintendents for Texas school districts. I didn't fit the profile, since I had not been either a vice principal (officially) or a principal. But because of my experience and training in California, I could have been. My passion led me toward serving language-minority kids—more mid-level, rather than executive level management.

What saved me, financially, after moving into the apartment was a job that I secured with the Bilingual Education Department at UT. I enjoyed the work, which included supporting bilingual student teachers, and I enjoyed the course work I had initially pursued under the scholarship the department had awarded me to earn my doctorate in bilingual special education. However, with Ernie's death, my options changed drastically: I could not spend four to five more years in school. I needed to get my degree and go to work at something that would pay what it would take to care for my son and send him to college. Getting accepted into the CSP program was the answer to a prayer.

Nolan Estes liked a lot of my other experiences too, such as my work with the councilman, and could see how I could transfer the skills I had attained to school leadership. Moreover, I had already successfully completed a year of graduate studies in the bilingual special education doctoral program. My potential to succeed in the CSP program was high. Once, when we had to introduce ourselves to a room full of superintendents who were attending a conference at a hotel in Austin, I gave my entire introduction in Spanish. Few of them understood what I had said, but I think I made my point. Some of the Hispanic CSP fellows were offended, but Dr. Estes was impressed. He also loved it when, from the back of the room, I verbally confronted a keynote speaker who had made some casual remark about civilization beginning in Europe. I was irate! There was a sea of white faces in that room— over five hundred school board members from across the state. I just couldn't let him get away with that kind of erroneous information.

I told him (and the audience) in a loud voice that one of the salient problems that minority students faced was the lack of accurate (or for that matter, any) information about the contributions of their ethnic groups in school textbooks. At that time, there were scarcely any stories about black or brown people in history, science, or literature books. That needed to change, I told him, so that those kids would not believe that their race was insignificant. They needed to read about their people's contribution to civilization just as white children did. Dr. Estes, who was standing near the podium, folded his arms and smiled.

There has been much improvement since then. I claim no credit, but publishers are doing much more these days to correct the problem of omission of diverse ethnic groups in school books.

I will forever be indebted to Dr. Estes for his vision of what I might become, in spite of my deficits in regards to requirements for admission to the program. This would be a two-year, fast-track PhD that I desperately needed, given the new responsibility I had received for taking care of Jonathan. I was a single mom without financial support. With the prestigious degree and guaranteed good job placement, I could quickly move on to work that would be satisfying and that paid the higher wages in my field. Although I would never serve in the superintendent's role, I would still benefit from the degree and would be able to serve Texas's children through employment with various departments of the Texas Education Agency (TEA): gifted education, special populations, and accountability.

Because of the generosity of Dr. Estes, UT, and the CSP, I had extraordinary opportunities to grow through international travel and exposure to countless acclaimed contemporary educational leaders at seminars and symposiums. For example, we CSP fellows traveled as a group to Europe in the spring of 1992. We visited Paris, Holland, Brussels, and several other small European countries. Before leaving, we wrote and published papers on significant school topics that we later presented before a huge audience of delegates to the Ninth International Conference on Technology and Education. The conference took place in Paris, France, in March 1992. My paper (which was written with a CSP colleague, Linda Reeves), "Moving toward Global Literacy with Technology,"[1] was published in the conference's compendium of papers.

Those experiences contributed much to the shaping of my ideals and higher personal and professional goals. And they fortified me with the tools I would need for the role of advocate that I, to this day, employ when opportunities are presented and when I deem it to be necessary. Additionally, I acquired training and functional expertise in the use of computers, software programs, and other technological knowledge associated with use of the Internet. These new skills accounted for a quantum leap in my list of professional competencies—competencies that opened numerous new doors for advanced employment, not to mention countless hours of personal entertainment and satisfaction. Until then, I'd never turned on a computer. Now I can't seem to turn mine off.

-James Hammond-

There were only four African Americans in the CSP program—three women (Mildred West, Sharon Jackson, and me) and one male,

---

1 Linda M. Reeves and Shirley Sprinkles, "Moving toward global literacy through technology," *The Ninth International Conference on Technology and Education I* (1992): 90–92.

James Hammond. We all came to the program from different regional areas of the country and possessed different backgrounds as educators. Being black in the program, however, was one thing we all had in common. It was a significant overlay to the total experience. Our survival, academically and emotionally, came to rely heavily on the bond we formed. It was our staunch determination to hang on and hang in until we reached the point of victory, which was graduation with our doctorate degrees *and* our sanity still in tact.

Many were the times when one or another of us was reduced to tears and despair during the two years we studied in the program. James was the rock on which we black females could always lean. I must mention him in my story because he was so central to my tenacity. I stayed in the game and in the program, in spite of problems on the home front, largely because James wouldn't let me quit.

I thought I was tough because I was older and had more experience behind me, but one day the pressure from what I perceived to be insensitive "white folks" got to me, and I broke down. James found me crying uncontrollably in the admin office. People were all around me, but no one stopped to ask what was wrong…further proof, I thought, that they just didn't care. I was ready to throw in the towel. *What was I doing here, anyway?* I thought. James was passing through at about that time. He stopped in front of me. Observing my tear-stained face, my drooped shoulders, and my generally depressed demeanor, he surmised, accurately, that I was miserable.

He didn't ask what was wrong; he just said, "Come on. Get your stuff, and come on."

He gently led me away from the crowded office (and my embarrassment) down the street to a nearby restaurant. He gave me his handkerchief and waited until I was through crying.

I honestly couldn't explain to him why I was so sad and upset—something just ached inside of me. That was all I knew. I had worked all night on a presentation, but when I'd given it before the class, they hadn't listened, not one bit. It was a report on screening strategies one should utilize before hiring potential employees. I had relied on the research of Peter Drucker, the famous industrial and business consultant. I had thought my classmates, future school district chiefs, would be very interested in learning what Drucker had to say. I had even drawn whimsical caricatures to illustrate each of his guiding principles. But apparently they were not interested. My classmates, who had listened intently and respectfully to the white guy whose presentation I'd followed, had just ignored *me*; they had talked to each other throughout my presentation. That had hurt. I really didn't like to be ignored, not by them nor by anyone. I told all of this to my friend, who patiently listened.

James looked me in the eye. He said, "Shirley, I understand. I've been where you are many a time in my life. I served in the military. I know how you feel. My advice to you is to just say, 'screw 'em!' Hold your head up high. Keep doing the good work that you do, and, Shirley, never let 'em see you sweat!"

Though I'd heard it before, I will never forget that advice given to me by a caring friend. I will never forget James. He's my "brotha'" to this very day!

-Dr. Deborah Nance-

Internship with TEA was a part of the CSP. We fellows received compensation for our work as data assistants and were given many privileges to research and learn the technologies of school leadership and accountability. It was here that I met and worked under Dr. Deborah Nance. A gorgeous, blonde, long-haired, and curvaceous woman, Deborah was equally brilliant, conscientious, and tenacious at her work. I admired her attention to detail and her sensitivity to children's educational needs. Dr. Nance was in charge of making sure that products disseminated by the agency were of the highest quality. She was passionate about her job. I worked under her twice during my tenure at TEA.

I left Deborah's division for a two-year period in which I coordinated a portion of the state's gifted and talented (GT) program, the Jacob K. Javits Project, under the direction of a new supervisor, Evelyn Hiatt—another brilliant woman. It was during this time that I wrote the state standards for the review of all districts' gifted and talented programs. Having had the experience of participating in district program reviews for years in California before coming to Texas, I found the task to be an easy one. "Evie," as she was affectionately called, was happy with the results of my efforts. Our standards became the monitoring model for all other educational programs; they remain so today.

My work in GT became the basis of research from which my dissertation evolved. While participating as a consultant in a local Javits project, one that was designed to train teachers to use a teaching methodology that was more amenable to the full academic development of gifted students, I wrote a qualitative, descriptive narrative dissertation entitled *Implementing a Complex Classroom Innovation: Process, Problems, and Potential.*[2] It was an organic study that evolved over a period of one and a half years. It featured six well-documented case studies. It was an illuminating study that demonstrated how teachers change (or don't change) their practice after receiving a substantial amount of training and with additional, informal but regular coaching of each other on the strategies and techniques they learned in the training sessions.

I observed and documented in my findings just how difficult it was for teachers who had originally been trained in traditional, teacher-centered methods to change their practice, even with focused new training. It was not easy for teachers in upper grades, who were concerned about students' performance on state-mandated assessments, to become more flexible and to risk practicing open-ended, student-centered instructional patterns; lower level teachers and younger teachers were more inclined to try new approaches.

Friends said my dissertation read like a novel! For sure, it was exhausting to write. I wrote a 432-page manuscript. It was wonderful. The paper was nominated for dissertation of the year by the chairperson of my committee, my beloved, Dr. Ben Harris, but it did not win.

When the Jacob K. Javits grant that I was in charge of expired, I returned to Dr. Nance's department as statewide director of the program that was titled, Site-Based Decision Making and Planning—a derivative of Senate Bill I, Site-Based Decision making. In

2   Shirley Sprinkles, *Implementing a Complex Classroom Innovation: Process, Problems, and Potential* (Ann Arbor, Mich.: University Microfilms, 1993).

that role, I traveled throughout the state with other agency colleagues teaching people to implement this new legislative mandate.

The most memorable event of my tenure in that TEA department—Site-Based Decision Making, Training and Support—was the opportunity Deborah Nance gave me to plan and execute the most celebrated gala in the agency's history—the awards program in which school districts from across the state were invited to Austin to receive large sums of money for their students' high performance on the state-mandated achievement test, the Texas Assessment of Academic Skills (TAAS).

I was placed in charge of planning the ceremony, which was to be held in the University of Texas Performing Arts Center. Along with a stellar committee from our division, I staged a gala program that wowed everyone who attended. Over three thousand people came. It was Hollywood all the way! There was live jazz music in the foyer, with people pausing to cut a jig now and then; colorful balloons and flowers were everywhere. And students were the platform speakers, not stuffy old administrators. People said it was refreshing and festive—for the first time. Although it was not a heralded fact, as quiet as it was kept, it was also the first time that a black person had been in charge of producing the ceremony. The commissioner of education, Lionel "Skip" Meno, paid a special visit to our division the following morning to congratulate Deborah and her supervisor, Dr. Reuben Olivares, on a fantastic event. She beamed and pointed him in my direction. I felt so proud. Dr. Olivares seemed to stand three feet taller that day.

In Texas, I worked for nearly five years at the state level, monitoring implementation of educational legislation. It was work that I'd have loved to have been able do in California but had no clear path to achieve. It was through the University of Texas and my PhD program that the opportunity to do this type of work was presented. I was good at it, and, to my delight, I felt like my work had impact beyond a single classroom. During my tenure as director of the Site-Based Decision Making and Planning Program, I saw the quality of education change drastically in Texas. Significant change took place in public schooling—an area where, especially for minority students, it couldn't have been more greatly needed.

When I initially arrived to begin working at TEA as an intern of the CSP program, I was placed in the Division of Accountability, the parent division to the Department of Site-based Decision Making, Training and Support. At that time, black students were, academically, performing at the bottom of the heap: math scores on state assessments in the past had been at the thirtieth percentile and sometimes below. Reading scores were only slightly better, and graduation rates were less than forty nine percent in many areas[3]. There were only a minimal number of students identified to receive gifted education services. Learning about these problems was very troubling to me, so much so, that I wrote a paper about the situation, which I considered submitting for publication in the training manual that our department was developing for the Texas School Improvement Initiative:

WHAT SHALL WE DO ABOUT THE MATH PERFORMANCE OF AFRICAN AMERICAN STUDENTS ON TAAS?

It is time to finally address the chronic and persistent problem of poor performance by Texas's African American students in mathematics. In spite of rhetoric to the contrary, the plain truth is that the students have not been taught the fundamentals of arithmetic, let alone higher ordered reasoning skills, in a manner that gets through to them. At last, high stakes testing is forcing educators throughout the state to intently focus on the curriculum and on instructional practices that impact this large subpopulation of students.

Accreditation ratings and, tangentially, state and federal dollars are at stake. With so much riding on raising the scores of our students' work, old attitudes and beliefsthe foundation of educational practiceswill have to be reexamined and changed in regard to the education of African American kids. It no longer suffices to pat them on the head and say "poor things, ain't it awful?" while white students in majority white schools make scores that establish high ratings. With

3   http://www.tea.state.tx.us/studentassessment/reporting/results/summary

campuses going on the TEA low-performing list due to the failure of African American students to meet minimum performance standards, there is a groundswell of concern among districts with high concentrations of black pupils, that is, at minimum, uncomfortable. Not only status but money is now on the line.

The concern is long overdue in the eyes of thoughtful, angry African American Texans, who have looked on for years as dismal published test scores have reflected the undereducation and the miseducation of their children. To their credit, the resulting frustration has been restrained and, so far, has not been taken to the street. What many parents of these students don't know is just how complex the problem is. Complications surrounding the educational experiences of a large majority of African American students in Texas schools are intertwined with a myriad of familiar political and economic problems that have long plagued the ethnic group in the larger society. The scope of the problem is extremely broad, encompassing issues ranging from teacher and administrator attitudes to inappropriate curriculum, from the inadequate preparation of teachers to the prejudicial hiring practices of many school districts. Important as they are, those issues will not be dealt with in this paper. Our discussion will focus more narrowly on possible ways to mitigate the pattern of failure of black students to meet minimum standards in math performance.

Much has been made among educators of the diverse learning styles of today's student population: a population that more and more reflects the growing black and brown complexion of the state. For the most part, though, there has been talk without action. While staff development dollars have been directed toward bringing forth new information and strategies to teachers about how African American students learn, as has been the tradition with most of the funds used for such training, little change actually occurs in the classroom, and the impact for students is minimal. It is widely known that teachers, for the most part, don't transfer what they learn in training to their classrooms.

They typically try out the new ideas for a short while, then, if the new methods don't fit with their personal belief system and teaching style, teachers abandon the newly taught methods, close the classroom door, and go back to doing what they've always done.

Teachers may find out that African Americans generally respond well to *relational* learning opportunities—that is to say, they grasp new concepts (including mathematical ones) more readily when they are presented using concrete or semi-concrete materials. And they may be told that new learning should be couched in preexisting knowledge and understandings that go to the experience base of the students themselves, rather than through highly irrelevant symbols and abstract, incomprehensible language. Teachers may know that personalized stories and familiar situations work best as a means of engaging these students interest and experientially learned knowledge (which is often vast) in mathematical problem-solving regardless of the grade level.

Knowing this, however, does little to change the practice of teachers who are clueless as to its application with black students. This is especially insidious in a state where two-thirds of the teachers of these students are white, and have had experiences that, for the most part, due to constraints imposed by social tradition, have been vastly different from those of African American students. It is a point not to be lost in the analysis of cause and effect. Sure, white teachers can be great math teachers, many are, but do they know what matters to black students? Do they understand how to make instruction *relevant* to them?

From a curriculum standpoint, educators would do well to consider the innate, natural strengths that African American students characteristically possess and display as a basis for the development of meaningful mathematical courses. Any serious observer of black children has to notice, for example, the incredible ingenuity and resourcefulness of these children. Their ability to successfully manipulate structures and systems to their advantage is the result of hundred of years of tradition and lessons in resiliency passed on to them by their ancestors. Every black child learns how to survive by manipulating, to some extent, his or her world. Some blacks refer to this ability as "hustle." Whites call it by more sophisticated names like "enterprising" and "streetwise." Either way, it involves understanding concepts that depict what it takes to participate in the game of life: supply and demand, costs versus benefits, services and products, etc.

African American students would greatly benefit by an approach to mathematics instruction that takes into account their inherent tendency and strong need to employ survival tactics. Such an approach would focus on the relationship between their grasp of key concepts and achievement in the mathematics discipline and their ability to survive in the global economy that confronts them now and (increasingly so) in the future.

By all accounts, implementation of such curricula would not be difficult. African American kids are not only highly motivated by capitalistic concepts, just like white kids are, but they have traditionally demonstrated considerable aptitude for grasping math that is associated with money. There is nothing wrong, in my opinion, with looking for solutions where they lie. A strong mini-economics curriculum that features a series of short but highly structured instructional units based on an entrepreneurial theme and that incorporates elements of simulation or play-acting could be part of the answer for African American students in grades kindergarten through twelve.

It's worth a try. What is there to lose?

Although blacks and Hispanics are still performing too far below their white counterparts, the picture today is nowhere near as bleak as it was, thanks, in large part, to the aggressive approach that people like "Skip" Meno, Deborah Nance, and Reubén Olivares took to monitoring quality in instruction and holding districts accountable for the progress of *all* of their students. They did this by disaggregating annual test data by ethnicity and socioeconomic status (taking into account economically disadvantaged students), analyzing results, eliminating inappropriate placement of minority students in special education, and requiring that plans for improvement that contained goals, benchmarks and timetables be submitted annually to the state agency for review and approval. These changes were not always well received, but they were changes that were long-overdue. I'm happy to have had a role in that change.

-Changing Focus, Changing Lifestyle-

In late October 1995, I answered an employment ad in the local newspaper that was recruiting a sales consultant to cover the south Texas territory for CTB/McGraw-Hill, a division of The McGraw-Hills Publishing Companies, Inc.—the largest publishing company in the world. Answering the ad was a random act, done purely on an impulse.

To make a long story short, I received a call inviting me to interview for the position. I accepted. After a brief interview two weeks later in the airport of Canton, Ohio (to which the company flew me), Richard "Rick" Dobbs, then CTB's national vice president of Marketing and Sales hired me. We met there in Ohio because Rick was en route to a meeting somewhere else. Since he had a brief layover in Canton, he hired me between flights! That's kind of the way things were in the publishing business, I would learn—always "on the go."

I became an assessment consultant, marketing and selling norm-referenced achievement tests to school districts, colleges, universities, and one-stop literacy programs throughout the south Texas territory. Much of the work involved teaching people about testing, its importance and how to use the results. I covered an area from Midland to Brownsville on the Mexican Border and from Waco to El Paso—in other words, a *huge* area.

In addition to gaining exceptional travel experiences throughout Texas, I attended training conferences and regional sales planning retreats in many other states that I probably would never have visited otherwise—Tennessee, Georgia, Colorado, and Missouri, to name a few—I enjoyed frequent trips to the U.S. Virgin Islands (which was part of my sales territory). I received excellent professional training as a presenter and a writer. Lord knows I had to write my share of reports and updates to marketing materials. And I was well paid in both salary and bonuses.

At last, I was able to afford to purchase another dream house. It is the one I live in today. I tell my friends, "It's between a condo and a ranch." That's a very good description of my home. After all, it does have a big, wooden, screened-in porch. Because of that, although it is really not all that large, I think of it as a real Texas-type home.

I'm also proud that I was able to recruit a black male consultant to cover the northern half of Texas for CTB. Few blacks are employed in the sales area of test publishing, though it is very lucrative work. Black male consultants are extremely rare. When I learned that this is because they seldom apply, I recruited a wonderful former high school principal who I knew in Austin, and Rick Dobbs also hired him. Eddie Orum was handsome, well spoken, smart, and well dressed. We were great partners, and we covered the entire state of Texas.

Eddie continues to work and is highly successful in Texas and two other states. As a national accounts consultant, he now heads a team of sales consultants, and (just between us) makes a boatload of money! "All things *are* possible to the courageous!"

Part VI

My Children

Your children are not your children. They are the sons and daughters of life's longing for itself.

—Khalil Gibran

Cheers, Tears, and Wings

Like most mothers, my highest, proudest achievement in life was giving birth and raising my children—and I raised four phenomenal children. I feel so very privileged to be called Mom by Bruce, Jonathan, Ellen, and Caryn. These are my pearls of life. Everyone who has known me for many years has observed the passion with which I have addressed my role of mother. Some have called me "super mom." I take exception to this title; I'm no super mom, but I have put a lot into the job—especially during my children's formative years. My efforts have not gone unrewarded. The children have all turned out great!

-Bruce-

My first child, Bruce, was born in Trenton, New Jersey, where Ken and I ended up living after leaving Los Angeles. He, unquestionably, received more of my time and attention during his earliest years than any of the other children did. He was a handsome, robust baby with long, sturdy limbs and a pleasant disposition. He was doted upon by a mother who was a former teacher and an incurable lover of little babies. Bruce did all of the developmental things early: he rolled over at six weeks, walked (without ever crawling) at nine months, and was talking fluently by thirteen months. I was in absolute awe of his every motion. I breastfed him, sang to him, read him nursery rhymes, played blocks on the floor with him, and cried when he got his first vaccination. He was my pride and joy. Caring for him filled many hours that might have been otherwise very lonely ones. He made me feel happy and fulfilled.

Growing up, Bruce reluctantly learned to share me with three siblings, but he still held on to as much of my attention as he possibly could. He did everything a curious, adventurous boy could do-stabbed himself in the leg with an ice pick while putting holes in a jar lid that contained his treasured captive moths, broke his father's tools, shot at birds with BB guns, tore tails off of lizards, and tried to drown his sisters in the family's swimming pool.

He also did many positive things: he was a cub scout, he studied martial arts, and, as a teenager, he took an interest in tropical fish and cultivated them in six large tanks that he scattered around the house. He worked in a tropical fish store after school in high school and developed a mini-business on the side as a consultant to people who owned aquariums and had sick fish. He started calling himself "Dr. Bruce." He even incorporated the self-appointed title in his signature. It was impressive.

Bruce learned to play tennis well—almost competently enough to play professionally. In high school, he played on a championship tennis team and got to travel to Hawaii for the final tournament. And he learned to love photography, an art form that he has continued to develop throughout his adult life and that he passionately pursues around the globe, winning prizes for his works.

Bruce's father, Kenneth, taught him high skills in leisure activities such as fishing and gardening. From Ken, Bruce also learned to build things and to accomplish numerous home improvement projects as well as to make common household repairs. Although, from my perspective, Ken may have lacked other desirable qualities, like good communication skills, Bruce could not have had a better father to teach him the "guy things." And he finally did learned to play the piano that I wanted him to learn—as an adult when he was ready to, not while I was paying hundreds of dollars toward this effort in his childhood! I guess it's true what they say about readiness: "When the pupil is ready, the teacher will step in."

Bruce was thirteen and in junior high school when Ken and I separated and divorced. It was a critical time in his maturation, and it was difficult this to be happening to his parents' and, indeed, to him. He was confused as to my reasons for leaving. He was too young to understand how I was feeling, and I tried not to let my hurt and anger spill over to my child. I needed for him to continue to love his father and to love me. When I left, I sat him down and gave him the option of coming with the girls (who were six and eight) and I or staying with his dad until he felt ready to join us. He opted to stay, fearing that his father would be too lonely by himself; Bruce wanted to take care of Ken. In his little heart, he felt sure this would blow over, and I would return—for his sake, if for no other reason. His mama, surely, would not leave him for too long. She'd come back.

That day never came. Within a year, I was talking about marrying some other dude, whom he barely knew. What a blow! Meanwhile, he had had opportunities aplenty to witness the relationship between his father and "the other woman" who had come between us and who took my absence as license to visit our home as she pleased. Bruce was caught up in a big web of confusion just when he needed stability most. Frustrated by this upheaval in his adolescent life, my child acted out his anger by withdrawing from me. He often behaved in obnoxious, juvenile ways whenever he was forced to be around his sisters, my new husband, Ernie, and me. He acted rude, recalcitrant, and selfish. Though I loved him to his core, more than once I had to "get tough" with him to bring him into line. Anger was acceptable, but respect was nonnegotiable.

Jonathan, Ernie's and my son, was born when Bruce was sixteen. He was still living with his father at the time of Jon's birth, but he moved into our home in Culver City about a year later when his father sold their home and moved to San Diego to work at a new job. Bruce had been my only boy child until his baby brother came along. On one hand, he was glad to have a little brother, but it was odd seeing his mom pregnant (and more than a little embarrassing when his friends were around). Once the baby was a reality, he adjusted to the idea a little better. Bruce would sometimes hold baby Jonathan and pack him around the house, but he was not absorbed with his little brother like the girls were. He took his role as big brother lightly. Besides, he thought that Ernie was overly protective of his young son.

When Ernie yelled at Bruce on one occasion for carelessly leaving the wall oven door open while Jonathan, the toddler, was riding his tricycle in the kitchen, Bruce took the reprimand very hard. His error had not been intentional, and Ernie had overreacted, in his opinion. Bruce was a sensitive child. He felt hurt and retreated from engaging with the family too much after that. He had friends and a girlfriend by the time Jon was big enough to really play with.

Before long, Bruce was off to college and out of our house. We didn't see much of him for a long while. This was partly because of school and partly because of a clash that took place between him and me at about that time. I literally gave him his "walking papers" when we couldn't come to terms with his behavior. Anyone who has raised a seventeen-year-old can probably identify with just how stubborn and unreliable kids can become at that age.

This was the problem I was facing with Bruce. He had a new car that his father had bought for him for graduation, and he was not available to do much work at all around the house after that; trash was left to rot in the garage week after week without getting set out for pick up, dirty dishes piled up in the sink and were spread all over the counter when it was his week to clean the kitchen, and his room was anything but clean. Every day I reminded him of his responsibilities, often yelling my disapproval. One day, I got tired of the way he just ignored my pleas. I wrote him a formal ultimatum, telling him to change his ways or find another place to live—a place where his behavior might be acceptable, because it no longer was in my house. It was Monday when I left the letter on his pillow. I gave him until Friday to shape up or move out.

I expected him to come to me and humbly apologize for his recalcitrant behavior and to start showing more effort. That is not what he did. He moved out.

Okay, I thought, *after a few days of suffering out there in those mean streets, he'll gladly come home and do right.*

I was wrong. Bruce had a part-time job as box boy at Gelson's Grocery Store in Beverly Hills. He had many celebrity customers. Among them was the female companion of Kareem Abdul Jabbar. She listened to Bruce's sob story about being put out of his home and offered him temporary quarters in their guest house. He accepted and moved in. He was *suffering*, all right! In essence, he thumbed his nose at my rules. He stayed there for a couple of months helping the young woman with chores and she and Kareem's child, until Kareem came off the road after the basketball season ended and told him he would no longer be needed. After that, another customer let him move into her small bachelor's apartment for a fraction of the rent. He kept going this way, living on his own and eating a lot of oatmeal, for a long time. In fact, Bruce never did return to our home, because, by the time he might have, it no longer existed.

A chasm caused by distance developed between the two boys (and, for that matter, between Bruce and the girls too) that is only now closing, since they are both grown men. Bruce was always interested in what Jonathan was doing, but the distance in miles between them put substantial distance in the growth of their relationship.

Although I don't mean to draw too many conclusions, I believe it is noteworthy to mention, as a point of observation, that the two boys experienced totally different fathering. Their fathers, Kenneth and Ernie, were light years apart psychologically and emotionally. Each boy was a byproduct of his father's parenting. It is a phenomenon that is observable to this day. Ernie was obsessed with Jonathan from the day he was born and throughout his lifetime. He was a warm, touching dad who doted on his boy. They wrestled on the floor, told jokes to each other, went sailing, played ball, went roller-skating, and huddled together on the sofa listening to good jazz late into the night until both fell asleep. Authors Oldham and Morris say this is typical parenting behavior of the mercurial personality. Jon adored his dad. They were best friends. They shared virtually everything.

Ken, by contrast, was involved in Bruce's development but did not occupy a central place in it in the same ways. His parenting style was more aloof and remote. Though he was watchful, he didn't manipulate the details of fathering in the same way that Ernie did. He was not a hugger; nor was he particularly playful. He held high expectations of all of his children—especially academically—but he was not what one would call a hands-on dad, unless there was an emergency. A sensitive child, like Bruce, could have benefited from more of Ernie's parenting style. He needed the security of knowing just how much his father really loved him. I believe he's still, at the age of forty-six, seeking that reassurance.

In spite of the difficulties he had dealing with mine and his father's divorce and our subsequent remarriages, Bruce forged ahead along his own path to make a life for himself that is a great deal more than average. He finished college in California with a major in business and a minor in real estate. He has capitalized on both. Thus far, he has worked his way up the corporate ladder to become vice president and major stockholder in his company, which specializes in leasing high-tech equipment. He owns five major pieces of real estate, including the tri-level five thousand square foot home he lives in out in Utah, and he is the CEO of a growing photography business. He has twice been named photographer-of-the-year in the annual swimsuit photography contest that is held in Cancun, Mexico.

I know I'm just bragging now, but allow me to tell you that Bruce is a great gourmet cook too. He has proven his prowess by three times winning top honors in the dessert division of the Real Men Cook, Too national cook-off. He's won his prizes with his scrumptious peach cobbler. He credits Mama, or Grammy, as he calls her, for his prize-winning recipe, but I know that pie tastes just like mine!

One thing Mama did teach him, however, was the importance of saving money. She vigorously preached thrift. Bruce was an attentive student. He religiously saved his allowance and any other money he received from work or for birthdays. At one time, he filled a large ten-gallon water jug with his extra change. He amused everyone by ironing his greenbacks until they were free of wrinkles and stacked up "pretty." We thought he was a basket case, but the habit has paid off in spades; he has amassed a good deal of personal wealth; he owns economic freedom in the truest since of the word.

Yet he is still frugal and conservative in his spending habits. In fact, the rest of us wish he'd loosen up a bit and throw a little of those coins our way! In fairness to my child, I will have to acknowledge his generosity in the outer realms of his life. He has been known to give expensive, very thoughtful gifts to people he cares about: uncles, aunts, cousins, and more than a few beautiful girlfriends. I'm comforted knowing that he really isn't a miser; he's just selective in his giving.

So far, he has not seen fit to marry. Living in Utah is a factor. First of all, there is the dominance of the Mormon religion and a culture to which he does not conform. He often speaks of his frustration with the seeming complacency of the young people there, especially the women. Bruce heads the marketing division of a large company that leases industrial equipment to manufacturers. He is a goals-driven individual who sets high standards for his own performance and expects the same of the people he works with.

As I understand it, he views most of the young women he comes in contact with (nearly 100 percent are white) as being resigned to accepting lifestyles that are far beneath what they could have. He describes their demeanor as "laid back" and economically "lethargic." Clearly, this is a rather judgmental assessment, but, nonetheless, it's his, and it is a source of irritation to Bruce. For example, he would like to see the young people (men and women alike) who he supervises at work aspire more aggressively to attain higher levels of financial success. He has seen the difference that hard work has made in his own life and passionately desires to help these young folks catch on to his way of thinking. Moreover, he is saddened by the amount of poverty that he witnesses in an otherwise wealthy culture. In his opinion, as expressed to me, poverty there rivals that of many inner cities. If he could do anything at all to reverse this, I believe he would. He devotes a fair amount of energy to this cause. So far, however, in regard to the women he has met in Utah, he has not become attached enough to marry one of them.

Secondly, the scarcity of black people in the state, particularly in Salt Lake City, where he lives, marginalizes his opportunities to select a mate matched to his own ethnicity and culture if he so desired. He has tried long distance relationships with black women; none of them have worked out. As a result, positively so, he has been forced to conduct his search with greater objectivity.

In fact, at the time of this writing, he does have a relationship with a potential partner with whom he has spent quality time for about three years. She is not from Utah, however. She isn't even American; she is from Czechoslovakia. She is a tall, slender, long-haired blonde, with a model-like figure. She possesses a strong work ethic and is highly attentive to Bruce. She cuddles, clings to, and assists him with virtually everything. Her adoration of him is highly visible whenever the family is together in the same place. He appears to have met his match in her. We are all waiting to see what happens. This relationship has lasted for three years, which is a record for him. If Bruce and his special lady do make the trip to the altar, my daughter-in-law will be welcomed into the family. She will not be the first white in-law in the family; Kenneth's second wife, Holly Brandon (whom he met and married after we divorced and with whom he had two more children), is also white. The marriage lasted about twenty years, but they are now divorced.

-Caryn-

When God thought I needed a good challenge, he gave me Caryn. Arriving in the world weighing eight pounds nine ounces, right from the start, Caryn came here to be noticed! Bruce was three and a half when Caryn came along. He was thrilled to have a baby sister. She was a "good" baby. She seldom cried and was always ready to give a gurgly, warm smile. Her chubby thighs, big bright eyes, and plump little cheeks were the focus of all our friends' attention.

Ken seemed happy to have a little girl to father. He made an adorable rocking cradle for her in the garage and painted it white. I was proud to lay her down in it and to show her off lying in her daddy's handiwork to visitors. When she was old enough to dance, he showed off her skills at every family gathering. She enjoyed his attention and loved pleasing him.

Caryn was a hope-to-die thumb-sucker. She found her thumb in the womb and enjoyed sucking it until she was almost six years old. It was a great pacifier. She was the sweetest, quietest little girl. What we couldn't understand was why she was content to sit down and not even *try* to crawl or to walk until she was nearly thirteen months old. She would play with anything we'd put within her reach, but she wouldn't allow her curiosity to push her toward things that were too far away. We carried her in our arms and pushed her in strollers for a long time. When she was ready, at thirteen months, she just stood up and walked. Just like that. That's pretty much the story of her life. Caryn marches to her own drummer.

Once she got her bearing, Caryn blossomed into a confident, though somewhat shy, little girl. She liked riding bikes, and, at one point, her father even bought her a mini-motorcycle. She didn't like dresses; she preferred the comfort and freedom of pants and T-shirts. It's fair to say that she spent a few years as a classic tomboy. I thought she should learn to play house and to enjoy dressing dolls, like I used to when I was a child, but to my utter dismay, the dolls I bought ended up baldheaded and naked. Caryn would wash and comb their hair until only a few strands were left. Then she would abandon them. I finally gave the dollhouse away. Playing with it just wasn't her thing.

While this may seem odd, in fairness, I must acknowledge that Caryn saw me in pants more than dresses in that stage of my life. In fact, it was pretty much the norm of the 1970s' culture. Women's lib was in full bloom, and pantsuits rapidly replaced dresses and skirts. All of Caryn's friends wore pants. It was "cool."

Caryn identified with me more than I really understood. She resembled me a great deal physically; her skin color, eyes, and mouth were a lot like mine. She was very attached to her mommy and would rarely stay with anyone else. When the other kids spent nights with cousins, Caryn would refuse to go. She always wanted to be near me. She and Ellen attended the elementary school where I taught in west LA. She loved being able to run up to me in the school yard and to know that I was just across the hall when she was in class. She was a good student, although she was very playful at times. Caryn had a handful of friends in elementary school who remain her closest friends to this day.

At one point, I cut Caryn's soft, crinkly, shoulder-length hair into a "natural" style. It was the short fuzzy style that was so popular in that day. I liked it; she hated it. At the time, I thought she liked looking more like me in that way. I wore a big "natural" that was easy to care for. All I had to do was wash it and wear it—no straightening or curling with a hot curling iron. She pretended to like it to please me, but she has since told me how much she didn't like her hair that short. She didn't think she looked enough like a girl, and she didn't like being mistaken for a boy. When she was old enough to manage her own hair, Caryn nursed and nurtured it until it grew way down her back. She has always worn long, silky hair ever since.

After sixth grade, Caryn's interest in school was diverted to her greater interest in boys. She was my first girl child, and I just didn't see what was coming. Adolescence caught me quite off guard. I was in for the ride of my life, and I had no saddle! Bruce had been easy. He had developed hobbies and experimented with tools like acetylene torches to kill flies that landed on the screen door—stupid stuff like that. This was different, very different. It was kind of like living with the main character in the movie, *The Exorcist*. There were mood swings, eye-rolling, secretive phone calls, and incessant picking on her younger sister.

This was also the time when our family was going through adjustment to my remarriage and the birth of a new child. All of this was more than overwhelming for Caryn. She missed her father's presence in her life, though she didn't complain too much out loud. Although she adored her new baby brother, Jonathan, when he came along, she was not nearly as taken with her new stepfather as I was, though she tried hard to fake it for a while. Eventually, in seventh grade, she started to unravel. Her grades went from good to bad and then to awful. She seemed to have lost her footing with the change to less structure in our home after I started working in the business, and there was no one person at school that she trusted and in whom she could confide her feelings, such as the teacher she'd adored in the sixth grade, Miss Jack.

I was pretty busy with a new marriage and the problems associated with keeping a new husband happy while juggling the demands of an expanding family, a new baby, and a teetering financial situation. I had to get back to work, and I took my eyes and, to a large degree, my *mind* off of Caryn. It was the wrong move. She needed my attention more than ever! I realized this when she began doing things around the house that were inappropriate and beyond her proprietary boundaries. An example of this was the occasion when I returned home early from the shop and found her perched on a ladder painting our fireplace a bright yellow. I nearly fainted! This was my favorite thing in the entire house, my beautiful, natural stone fireplace, and she had painted it yellow without consulting me first. Her motives were well intended; she just wanted to surprise me by brightening up what she perceived to be an outdated living room. She hadn't meant to make me angry, but anger was exactly what I felt. It wouldn't have crossed my *last year's mind* to do something as brazen as that in *my* mama's house! I backed out of the front door and went for a long drive to cool off. It was the first but not the last incident that sent up flares that signaled trouble in the making. Taking my attention off of Caryn at such a critical time in her life was, indeed, the wrong move. The mistake had irreversible consequences. It was one that I've lived to regret over and over again.

By the end of her junior high days, Caryn had seared the nerves of every member of our family with her adolescent behavior. In typical teenage fashion, she was clearly acting out, rebelliously, her feelings of emotional abandonment and of helpless entrapment. She trashed the bedroom she shared with her sister, laid her clothing and other belongings all over the house, and could not be counted on to complete any assigned chores. Much of this behavior characterized her age and stage: adolescence.

We held family meetings around the kitchen table every week to air concerns and to dole out deserved kudos as they occurred. Ernie and I thought this would give our blended family a chance to thrive—that, at a minimum, it would foster good, free-flowing communication. Instead, the meetings invariably turned into gripe sessions in which Caryn was the target of everyone's complaints. She felt attacked and stopped participating in the meetings. That process went nowhere.

Things worsened. Eventually, Caryn wrote me a note in which she expressed her desire to move to San Diego where her father was then residing and to be allowed to live with him. She told me that she loved me dearly but could not stand my husband. She felt this way largely because Ernie began picking up and locking away her clothes that he found lying around on the floor and in common family areas. His strategy was designed to make her appreciate her things more and to change her careless habit. But her hostility, especially toward him, only intensified. Now she was asking to be let out of this setting. Exhausted by all the drama and not having a better solution to the problem, I agreed to let her go. I believed that reconnecting with her father was probably a biological need as much as an emotional one. He had been quite remote in his demeanor after the divorce—only seeing the girls when they were dropped off for a weekend visit now and then, since there was no formal visitation order in place.

Perhaps, I thought, *he will be more effective than we are in reversing the downward spiral that we've been experiencing.* It was worth a try.

I was wrong; profoundly wrong—again.

After spending a year living with her dad and attending high school in San Diego, Caryn decided to return to LA to resume living with us. Things had not turned out as she had hoped. Her father was preoccupied with a new romantic partner and spent virtually no time at home with his daughter. He gave her more money to spend than she needed, a fully stocked refrigerator, and the keys to his car (although she had did not have a driver's license). But, what she wanted most—attention—was very scarce. Thankfully, she chose a set of friends, mostly girls, who were from good homes and who were on positive tracks. I shudder to think what could have happened if her buddies had been the opposite types.

Home was not looking like such a bad place after all. We missed Caryn, and she missed us. We welcomed her return, but precious time had been lost. Getting back into the mainstream of high school life in Culver City was more difficult than anyone had anticipated. Caryn had done reasonably well academically in San Diego, largely because she was afraid to cross her dad. But, the transition back into our home environment, where we were economically strapped and strug-gling to stay afloat, was more than that fifteen-year-old could handle. All of that and a profound loss of the freedom that she had grown accustomed to in San Diego took its toll. She began skipping classes (though she would go to school daily), and she grew increasingly more interested in getting the attention of men—not just school-aged boys. Once her head started to go down that path, school was just not all that important to her. She failed classes and lost credits for graduation.

When the end of the school year was looming and she realized she would not be marching with her friends, she took the GED exam and left school. My heart ached. She was out of control, and, to a large degree, it was my fault. I should have seen this coming and done something about it.

Armed with just a GED, Caryn was able to gain acceptance into Brooks College of Design, which was located in Long Beach, Califor-nia, next door to Long Beach State College. In fact, she was awarded a scholarship that paid her room and board as well as some tuition. She borrowed the rest in student loans.

By now, Ernie and I had separated; the house had been lost; Bruce had moved out on his own; and Ellen, Jonathan, Caryn (when she was home from school) and I were new residents in Mama's upstairs duplex apartment. It was small, dingy, and outdated in lots of ways. My king-sized bed was in the front room. All three children had to share the one bedroom. Things were significantly different, to say the least. Caryn hated our new place. She could not see how we could all live there. There was only one bathroom! She was ashamed to invite her friends in. Staying on campus was her salvation. At least, that's what she thought at the time.

Every weekend, I had the task of driving to Long Beach to pick her up and to return her to school on Sunday night. Time at home was largely spent planning how to get out with her friends. She was the party girl. We constantly fought over her lifestyle. She spent virtually no time at home with us and did precious little of the work to maintain order in the place. At the end of the school year, Caryn's grades were not very good. She lost her scholarship and owed a ton of money in student loans. She decided to get a job. She also decided not to come home (but that decision would be short-lived).

Instead, she moved into a modern apartment with two of her former high school friends. They agreed to split a rental fee of six hundred dollars a month. She got a job with a cosmetics firm that paid her well. She was on her own, at last—or so she thought. Within three or four months, Caryn lost the job she treasured so much. She was no longer able to make her financial contribution to the apartment that she shared with her friends. The other two girls soon moved out to another place, leaving Caryn to fend for herself without any money. The girls had enjoyed a few months of youthful freedom—answering to no one and entertaining friends and boyfriends. It had been exhilarating. But like a burst balloon, it had deflated all too quickly. It was over. Caryn was miserable. She would never be the same. She tried to hang on alone in the apartment, anything to keep from going home, but, needless to say, this didn't last long. She looked to me for help. I told her that I wasn't paying that much money for my own place and I *certainly* wasn't going to pay it for hers. Her only option was to come back home and live with us, once again.

At the end of summer, Ken invited Caryn to move back to San Diego to live with him and his new wife, Holly, and go to college. He really wanted all of his children to get a college degree. She accepted. Soon she was back in his home, taking courses at the junior college. She got another job, this time marketing cable TV in a lucrative area of the city. She was highly successful at this line of work, from time to time winning prizes and bonuses for surpassing her quarterly goals. She was also dating sailors, who were heavily populous in the city because there was a large naval base there.

Soon, too soon, she found herself pregnant with her first child. She was twenty-one, and she had not yet finished any of her schooling. Caryn was determined to stay in San Diego, so she moved out of her father's house into her own tiny apartment. She bought a few pieces of furniture and began to prepare for a new life that would include a small infant.

By the time baby Brandon Carrera was born, his father was long gone, and Caryn was alone, beginning the life of a single mom. Though she initially had some help from me, her stepmother, father, and friends, it soon became apparent that Caryn was not going to be able to work and care for her baby without substantially more support. Her father had started a new family and had his hands full with a toddler of his own.

Though Kenneth proudly welcomed his handsome first grandchild, his disappointment about the circumstances of Brandon's birth was thinly veiled. In fact, there was disappointment enough to go around. Our entire family felt the shockwave. We had all hoped that Caryn would graduate from college and find more solid footing before she started a family. Mama was beside herself. As for my part, I adored the baby, but I can tell you frankly that I was terrified of the future I saw for him. I was getting more stable, but I could not offer a lot of financial support just yet. After trying other alternatives that did not work out, we decided that Caryn and the baby should move in with me until things were more stabilized.

Caryn (of course) resisted, but I insisted. Timing could not have been better. Ellen had graduated from high school and was on her way to the University of Colorado. Jon was with Ernie up north in Oxnard. It was the perfect arrangement. Caryn moved into the little bedroom, and we made a temporary nursery in the small, enclosed alcove on the front of the house for Brandon. His "bassinet" was a pillow-lined dresser drawer. I continued to sleep in the front room. It was a makeshift living arrangement, at best, but it worked for the time being. Best of all, Mama was downstairs ready to lend a hand whenever we needed her.

When I moved to Moreno Valley, the apartment above Mama's became home to Caryn. She had it all to herself. In time, she placed Brandon in a good nursery/ preschool center nearby and went to work for A&M Records. It was her introduction to the world of music—a world she would return to again and again. Over time, she tried other types of employment, but she was unemployed by the time I was ready to leave for Texas.

I invited Caryn to move into my lovely cottage home out there east of LA and try to establish herself in a new job. She could go to school, work part time, and pay a portion of the house note as rent. I would pay the rest. She agreed and moved in. That arrangement seemed fine at first, but it didn't last.

Caryn never was able to find suitable employment in Moreno Valley; therefore, she was unable to pay any rent. In addition, she felt isolated. She longed for her friends in Los Angeles and was disinterested in the upkeep of the house. Thus, the house was not receiving the care I expected, and its deterioration was costly. When I saw that this was not helping any of us, I terminated the arrangement, and Caryn moved back to LA, this time to live with her aunt, Sarah, for a short while.

Eventually, Caryn and Brandon moved back to Mama's upstairs apartment. Mama loved having her great grandchild so close. She was a godsend to Caryn, providing both care and grandmotherly love to Brandon. She taught him many things: how to count, how to read, and how to play many games. She doted on both of them—especially in the area of cooking for them. Things were going along fine. Caryn worked, dated, went out with friends, and generally enjoyed her single life. Having a loving support person close by made things a lot easier.

When little Brandon was five years old, his mother gave birth to a second son, Merricks. Once again, Caryn had to stop working. Now she had two young children to care for—alone. Life, under these circumstances, took on new dimensions. She was overwhelmed. Her responsibilities were heavy, and her resources were minimal. But this was not to be the end.

Five years later, little Colin was born. He completed the family that she now has: three sons, all five years apart.

You might be asking by now, "Why are you telling about this? What does your daughter's life have to do with your own?"

The answer is: everything! Our lives are deeply intertwined. It's just the way it is.

When I was a mother of young children, I had no idea how long I would have this job of mothering my children. I thought they would grow up, get married, have their own children, and I would just visit with them and enjoy spoiling my grandchildren. That was the "American story" I had seen played out on TV. I had no idea that my life (and my financial resources) would unfold in tandem with the lives of my children.

Whenever Caryn found herself in a pickle, I was not just a silent spectator; I was thrust into the situation too. Every parent understands this. We just can't stand by and watch our offspring in trouble without jumping in to help. That is what I have done for all of nineteen years—*help*.

My ear has stayed pressed to the ground, listening for all signals of distress from California. Months of rent money, car repairs, and just plain atta-girl bucks have left my own hands for my daughter's. This is not a complaint. I have willingly aided her through tough times.

There have been windows of time when Caryn has caught her balance, and she did not seek nor need my help. I've encouraged her quest toward self-reliance. The journey has been a rugged one, but it continues nonetheless. The distance between Texas and California in miles is great, but we shorten it through frequent telephone conversations, sometimes lasting for hours.

I know as I write this that many parents, grandparents, aunts and uncles, and sisters and brothers can identify with this story.

The good news that I want to end with is that Caryn's battle to survive has reaped benefits that can't be measured on any scale known to man. Out of it has come a strong, determined woman and head-of-household. Caryn has learned the hard way how to manipulate conditions to favor her survival needs and to use every means available to her to secure her little family. The annals of history are replete with stories about women like my Caryn—women who refuse to believe in failure, women who just won't give up or give in to poverty, no matter how relentlessly it stalks them. At age forty-two, she has achieved her first college degree (an associate of arts) with the higher ambition of getting a bachelor's degree and after that a master's degree of her own. Am I proud? You bet I am!

She has earned my respect for her tenacity. In the (paraphrased) words of Booker T. Washington: The true measure of success is not what one has achieved but the number of obstacles one has overcome.[1]

My greatest challenge today, in regards to my daughter, is to just keep my mouth shut and my hands in my pocket! "Fools rush in where angels fear to tread" is an expression I've always heard but only now understand, thanks to my daughter. Like me, in time, she'll figure it all out.

My fondest wish for Caryn and the boys, as I get older, is that they will move in my direction so we can be closer physically. I am grateful, in the meantime, for every minute of telecommunicated time that we spend together. I take every opportunity to mail, email, and call in order to maintain our relationship. They are precious to me! It is said that time changes all things. I am hopeful that time will bring us closer.

-Ellen-

From the moment I announced that I was pregnant with our third child, my husband, Kenneth, began distancing himself from me. We stopped having intimate relations and all pretenses that we were a happy couple were dropped. I was working as a teacher when I found out about Ellen's impending birth, so I finished out the semester; then I went home to await the blessed event.

I was elated. I had always dreamed of having a large family, similar to the family that I experienced when I visited my beloved Aunt Dolly

---

1   Quote DB, http://www.quotedb.com/authors/books/booker-t-washington.

(Daddy's sister, Minnie Lee) in Texas. She was my role model of the ideal mother. I loved being a mother, and I adored my children. My marital partner, however, felt differently about the subject of children. Unfortunately, it was not something we had had one minute of serious discussion about prior to or during our marriage. It was not until I was eight months into the pregnancy with Ellen that Ken made his true feelings clear. In no uncertain terms, he told me that he really didn't want a baby; what he really wanted was a boat. I think I know what he meant: we already had two young children. Supporting an even larger family would add additional responsibility that would consume all of his discretionary income and cause the postponement of his dream of owning a boat for fishing—his favorite hobby. Yes, I knew exactly what he meant, but it was the wrong way and the wrong time to say it.

When I think about that conversation today, as I see our beautiful and talented daughter moving about in her life so competently fulfilling her dreams and ably shouldering the responsibilities of career and motherhood, I smile. Little did he (or I) realize what a true blessing Ellen would turn out to be for the both of us and for our entire family. At the time, though, his words pierced my heart, as any expectant mother can understand.

So fragmented was our relationship by that February day when I gave birth that, after staying through my labor to see what the baby's gender would be, her father left the hospital and stayed away for two days, until it was time to take me home. On that day when, due to pressure from the hospital to complete the birth certificate, we had to give our child a name, he blurted out the name, Ellen. Since she was born on Mama's birthday, February tenth, I gave her the middle name Copply.

From the beginning, Ellen Copply was a beautiful, petite, demanding child, who cried all the time. Though I had nursed the two older children successfully, I had difficulty keeping up a good supply of breast milk for this one. I'm sure the level of stress I was processing didn't help. Anyway, her feeding needs were not being met. She screamed endlessly for the first three months. Unlike her siblings, she did not thrive into a robust, happy infant until I conceded that breast-feeding was not working and placed her on a commercial formula.

Nowadays, when she's stubborn, I attribute it to the fact that she drank cow's milk instead of mine.

In a short time, Ken came to see how wrong he had been about his baby daughter's conception. She grew on him rather rapidly and soon became the proverbial apple of his eye, just like her sister, Caryn, had been when she was born. I'd like to say I forgot about his remark, but I didn't. The very last thing I did before we separated for good was to help him purchase his beloved boat.

Ellen was young when we divorced. She didn't seem quite as affected by separation from her father as did Caryn. She genuinely tried to adapt to her new stepfather. She was beginning to show signs of incorporating the "pleaser" traits of a conscientious personality type.

Ellen pursued school seriously and got good grades all the way. She made a lot of friends in school. They were a good mixture of ethnically diverse kids that she is still connected to. Her social life was not brisk but interesting. When she was invited to escort a young man to his beautillion, I made a long, turquoise lace and satin gown, which she wore very elegantly over her tall, thin figure. She was so proud to tell people that her mom made her dress. Actually, it was the only solution I could afford.

Ellen worked at a few babysitting jobs growing up and later did full-time work in a couple of retail stores in the area. Her vibrant personality was cultivated in these experiences. They assisted her in the development of good people skills. She graduated from Culver City High, where she had participated in the Mentally Gifted Minors program and was accepted into the School of Journalism at the University of Colorado at Boulder. She became interested in sports journalism and was fortunate to make some great connections with people who were prominent in the sports world.

At one point while a student at UC, Ellen was awarded an internship with the San Diego Chargers. Her excellent work ethic did not go unnoticed. Upon graduation, she was interviewed for and hired into a coordinator's position with the National Football League in New York City. It was her first time in the Big Apple, and she began operating in the "big league." I was paranoid, at first, to think that my baby girl was all alone in a place that had the potential to swallow her up and spit her out. I crossed my fingers and prayed a lot.

In spite of my trepidation, Ellen did just great. She had learned very well how to be on her own during the time she spent in Boulder. Within a year, she left the NFL and landed a job with the National Basketball Association as a media coordinator. The glitz and glamour didn't change my girl. She stayed focused and did good work.

Her brothers couldn't have been happier with her career choice—they got tickets and good seats at all the NBA playoffs. They both have many pieces of memorabilia and a lot of souvenir photos with sports megastars. Their trophies and sports paraphernalia are proud possessions, to put it mildly.

I will always be glad that Ellen stayed and struggled through the bad times with me.

I used to tell her, "It may look bad now, sweetheart, but it won't be that way always."

She watched me work hard and sympathized with me while I stayed up until early hours of the morning completing coursework for my master's degree. Sometimes, she would get out of bed and offer to type for me. My painfully slow typing was annoying to her ears, especially when she was trying to sleep just ten feet away.

We got to know each other more intimately than did Caryn and I because of this. Ellen became acquainted with my friends, and they with her. She celebrated my victories with me, and because I was receiving poverty-level income, she was eligible for a variety of college grants, including the Pell Grant. We were a blessing to each other. God is both just and merciful.

Today, Ellen resides in Orlando, Florida. She is recently divorced from her husband, Cedric Calhoun, but they love and equally share in the care of their two beautiful young children, Chloe and Marcellus. Ellen works in the "world's happiest place," Disney World. She was hired to direct programs associated with sports in the World Sports Complex, but she has since moved into other areas of employment with the corporation. Ellen lives a magical life now compared to how it all began.

Additionally, she goes out of her way, using her excellent coordination skills, to plan and implement events like family reunions that serve to weave the entire family together. She has carved out a special place in the lives of many friends as well as family. As is true with her sister and the rest of us, Ellen's life lessons continue to unfold day by day, year by year. She, too, is figuring it all out.

Out of all my children, Ellen shares with me the relationship that is the most intense and probably the most authentic. We are both high-achieving, conscientious women, who bristle at the hint of criticism. This is a personality flaw that we are both trying to overcome. Ellen is my favorite sounding board. Her rational, analytical mind can spin things that I'm contemplating in such a way that enables me to see them through a whole different light. We are both stubborn and each frequently accuses the other of being opinionated. It's the yin and yang of our relationship. I get in her face when I think I need to; she gets in mine for the same reason. Yet, when the situation is serious, she's the first to leap to my side, and I to hers. Sometimes this tendency gets a little out of hand.

For example, Ellen called my current husband, Leo, in North Carolina when she learned of our wedding plans and grilled him extensively about his intentions. (I had told him to expect a call from "Marcia Clark," the famed, crisp-tongued, prosecuting attorney of the O. J. Simpson trial. He needed to be warned about what to expect.) It's a wonder we ever married at all after her performance. She was then, and remains to this day, fiercely protective of her mama.

-Jonathan-

If ever a child was kissed by an angel before departing baby heaven, it must have been Jonathan Sprinkles. The cuddly, calm-natured, honey-skinned child we called Jon was born early in the second year of mine and Ernie's marriage. No child could ever have been more adored. Ernie was beside himself with pride. By then, he had celebrated his forty-sixth birthday and was having his dream fulfilled. He named his son Jonathan after the fabled high-soaring seagull. The significance of this birth had many ramifications, most of which I could not grasp at the time. Now Ernie had three sons; Mark, who was a son from a previous relationship, and Brian, his son from his first marriage, were already teenagers.

Certainly, Jon was our love child, but he was more—much more to the family. He was the new centerpiece of the neighborhood. In addition to his five siblings, Bruce, Brian, Lisa, Caryn, and Ellen (Mark would enter his life much later), Jon was the adored baby of every of his sisters' girlfriends and boyfriends in the neighborhood. They routinely came to the house after school to hold him. Our house was a favorite gathering place, and Jonathan was the main attraction for a long time. That kind of love and a doting father established the foundation of little Jon's life. He thrived on the attention that was lavished on him from all quarters.

Moreover, he and I were constant companions. He went every-where I went—even to work at a daycare center, cozily nestled in a toddler backpack on my back. I enjoyed nurturing this, my last, child. I was thirty-nine years old when he was born, and I would not be giving birth again. As I was older, I brought wisdom and more patience to the task of mothering this child. They were virtues that worked to his advantage. I took my time fostering his development; he was not rushed through any of his stages. His father endorsed and encouraged my attentiveness to him, and he pursued the same course.

(Years later, after Jon had grown up, when he and I were together and observed my daughters breastfeeding their children, he often turned to me to ask about the time when he was an infant.

"Mom, how long did you say you breastfed me?" he would ask.

Then when I would tell him the truth—two and a half years—he would turn every color of embarrassed and scream, "Oh, my God!"

This was a joke between us.

I would then take advantage of his embarrassment to add, "My only requirement was that you wean before going to college."

Then would come the wail: "Ma-a-a-a-a-!")

Ernie and I separated when Jon was five years old. The pressures of blending families with rebellious teenage children and the weak performance of our business catapulted us into an abyss of debt and disappointment that was more than we could take. As soon as he found a place for himself, Ernie asked to take Jon. At that time, our relationship was broken but not severed. I had my hands full with Caryn and a house that was threatening to become a foreclosure. I knew how much Ernie adored his son. I felt certain that he would do everything in his power to care for him as carefully as he thought I would. So, I said "All right, you've got it!"

I've never regretted that decision. It was a good one. When we divorced, three years later, we settled on joint custody of Jonathan.

Jonathan lived with his father for eight years. They were the "dynamic duo." Anywhere Ernie was, Jon was there too. They bonded in the most special way. They were not just father and son; they were best friends who goofed around together and traveled together whenever the opportunity was presented. Ernie freely hugged and loved his son, unabashedly showing his affection. He loved his son unconditionally. Always, he expressed his wish for him to become the "best person he could be." To this day, Jon tries hard to live up to his father's admonition.

When Jonathan was fifteen years old, his father died of cancer. Just prior to his death, when he was too sick to carry on with a dependent child, Ernie sent Jon to live in my care in Texas where I was attending school. It was the hardest things Jon ever had to do. I can't imagine what it must have been like to have to pack up and leave all of your friends and your sick best friend who was also your father overnight on Christmas Day. To say it was a painful transition of cataclysmic proportions to the young boy would be tantamount to trivializing the most pivotal experience of his life. While he was not exactly traumatized (he was, after all, going to his own mother), Jon was greatly challenged to adjust to the revolutionary changes that were required to live within a household of a whole new set of folks that might become his new family. He was not a happy camper. To his credit, he made the best of a bad situation.

After his father's death, Jon seemed more determined to fulfill Ernie's wish for his son to "Be the best that you can be." He moved back to Texas; came to grips with the idea that he would not be returning to Los Angeles or Oxnard, California, where he'd lived with Ernie; and consciously tried to fit in at school in Austin. He attended high school and took part in as many activities as he could, including becoming the school's mascot at athletic events. Making people laugh was something he enjoyed and was very good at doing. He was daring and creative along these lines. The students liked him and encouraged his antics with laughter and applause. The experience was seminal; Jon would later decide to make his living entertaining people.

Jonathan went on to the University of Texas after high school where he was the recipient of a full four-year scholarship. There he blossomed as a student-activist and scholar. He organized the first African American male students' support group, which focused on doing positive things to improve the community, scholastic achievement, and campus life. His leadership skills became obvious to all observers. He received many recognition awards, including the Barbara Jordan Leadership Award, the Outstanding African American Student Leadership Award, and the distinguished honor of being named to the Dean's Dozen list, representing one of twelve highest performing seniors. To say I was proud would definitely be an understatement!

Jonathan lived in a dorm on the campus during those four years, although he came home regularly on weekends to do laundry and eat Mama's home cooking. He was my baby boy, and I was always glad to see him darken our doorstep.

After graduation from college, Jonathan was hired into the marketing and sales division of Dell, Inc. He took his new position seriously. He left for work every day dressed as if he owned Dell! He used his earnings to invest in handsome suits, ties, and shirts. Before long, he had established a reputation for elegant dressing. It was a reputation that had been passed on from his father—a legacy of sorts in which he took great pride. He definitely captured the attention of his superiors as a "comer." Soon he was promoted to handling high-dollar corporate accounts—*really* high.

Jon did very well in this field, but his heart was really in public speaking. In fact, he joined the Dell Toastmasters group, and in relatively short time, after winning multiple lesser speaking competitions, finally earned the title of International Toastmaster of the Year. Demand for his speeches became so great that he was forced to transition from working for Dell to starting his own speaking enterprise. As he tells it in his talks, "It was either quit or get fired because I was away from the job so much."

It was a quantum leap—one fraught with anxiety and trepidation at first. Little by little, Jon learned about a whole new world out there called motivational and inspirational speaking.

Like a good student, Jon pursued knowledge about his chosen career, and found out just how lucrative it could be if one were good and if one had a message that people wanted to hear. Jon has diligently worked to become one of the top speakers in the country. He's well on his way to that goal. Check him out at http://www.jsprinkles.com.

Following his father's admonition, Jonathan Sprinkles wants to be "the best speaker that he can be." Today he is in high demand. He crisscrosses the country, delivering on average one hundred to two hundred speeches a year to crowds that are growing ever larger. There's little doubt where my son got his "gift for gab," but the difference is, he gets paid for his!

Jon is the most spiritually-driven of all my children. He was baptized into the church he attends eight years ago. He is devout in worshipping, giving, and serving there. When the church relocated to Houston, he moved away from Austin and bought a condo there to be able to maintain his affiliation. It is not unusual for me to search for Jonathan when he is visiting in our home only to find him in deep meditation or quietly reading scriptures out on our back porch. I'm amazed at how this aspect of his development took root and grows more deeply as he gets older—amazed, but pleased.

This is my affectionate, thoughtful child. There's always one who loves a good, long hug and never fails to kiss you goodbye when he leaves. That's my Jonathan. When I was working on my doctorate and he was in high school, he used to quietly take my glasses off whenever I fell asleep reading. He would lay them on the nightstand, gently slip my book out of my hand, and turn off the light. Jon never misses an opportunity to send or bring me something special on those special occasions in my life: he always remembers Mother's Day, birthdays, and Christmas. His gifts are unique, always something that he has observed that I either need or like (except chocolate candy) and always beautifully packaged. What's not to love about a child like that?

Someday, hopefully someday soon, he will find a lovely and equally wonderful young lady on whom he will lavish that kind of love and attention. When he does, she will be a lucky one! He has the makings of a very special husband—similar, in the positive ways, to his dad.

Part VII

My Life Today

If you want to lift yourself up, lift up someone else.
—Booker T. Washington

Third Marriage

-Leo Morris-

At sixty-three years old, I met and married my current husband. He's a great guy, whose values, energy, and life-direction coincide with mine. I just love him to pieces! Now don't I sound like a real Texan? My new love and I met right in my own home, which was just where I've told my friends for years that I would have to meet any future husband, because the job with McGraw-Hill afforded me little time to socialize locally, and there were no, I mean *no* African American men among the people I met while working.

Cardette Carroll, a friend of mine and Leo Morris's sister, introduced him to me one day when she was in my home visiting and writing a long Christmas letter by hand that she had asked me to type on my computer when it was finished. She informed me that her brother, Leo, would be coming by soon. Since he lived in North Carolina and was only in town for the holidays, he was staying with her, but she had the house key in her possession, so he would be stopping by to retrieve it.

When the doorbell rang, she answered the door and ushered a short, well-built, dark-skinned man into the small family room where we had been sitting before a toasty, warm fire that burned brightly in the fireplace. He came bouncing in, all five feet of him, full of smiles. He extended his hand to give me a warm handshake. Since Cardette was still writing, I pulled up an extra chair for Leo across from me in front of the fireplace. We began to make small talk, which steadily progressed into mirthful conversation.

"So, I hear you've built an addition to your home." He had heard this from his sister.

"Yes," I replied, "it is the love of my life. Would you like to see my new porch?"

He acted excited about seeing what I'd just had done on the back of my house. Once outside on the new wooden porch, his eyes expanded to the size of saucers. "Wow," he exclaimed, "This is fantastic! How did you ever come up with this idea?"

I told him how I had designed and built the wood and screen outdoor room as an addition to the back of my house, next to the patio that had a vine covered pergola. With the help of a great architect who accurately grasped my desires and designed just what I described, the room turned out to be a perfect haven for sheltered relaxation in all types of weather. The eighteen-by-twenty-two-foot room that is accessed through French doors leading from the living room features a high cathedral ceiling with wooden beams and a ceiling fan that keeps the space cool in summer. There is inset, specially coated screening all the way around three of its sides, ceiling-to-floor. The wooden decked floor extends beyond the room to the outside deck, which is accessed from two screen doors and where a portable barbecue pit sits. Furnishings for the space include several cushioned patio chairs, a glass-top table with bar stools, plant stands, and small social tables. Twelve to fifteen people can be comfortably accommodated on the porch at any given time.

"I built this place for my mama," I told him. "I can't wait till she gets here to see it. I even bought this rocking chair for her so she won't have to sit outside and fight the mosquitoes."

"She will love it," he reassured me.

Back inside, we laughed, joked, and shared some serious thoughts on a variety of subjects, from music to the stock market, while his sister ignored us in favor of completing her long, long letter. Before we knew it, more than an hour had passed. What I thought was going to be a long wait turned out to be too short for the two of us. We instantly liked each other. Before leaving, Leo asked for permission to call me from North Carolina some time just to chat. He said he had thoroughly enjoyed the visit. I complied and gave him my phone number, stating that I looked forward to hearing from him. I thought that was the end of the story, but I was wrong. In fact, it was just the beginning.

The very next morning I received a phone call at around 8:00

a.m. It was Leo. "I'm in San Antonio. We usually have our family's Christmas dinner here with my aunt and uncle. I've asked them for permission to invite you to join us if you can. Is it possible for you to clear your calendar to ride down here with Cardette today? I'd really love having you as my guest."

I was stunned but flattered. It was Saturday, and my "calendar" consisted of all the things I least wanted to do: take out the trash, do the laundry, and dust the ceiling fans. I graciously accepted the invitation and picked out something festive to wear. The day turned out marvelously. We kibitzed back and forth about how I got to San Antonio. Playfully, we held hands under the table. His excitement was very thinly veiled.

He had told his Uncle Richard before I arrived, "I think I went to Austin and fell in love."

Uncle Richard had replied, "Again?"

This remark is a standing joke in our household.

As fate would have it, Leo's flight from San Antonio to Raleigh was canceled the next day due to a freak ice storm. He took this as an opportunity to catch a bus and return to Austin for one last visit with me.

I was shocked to hear that he was returning so soon, but, as it turned out, his instincts were right on the money. We continued our playful banter, turning it, eventually into romantic exploration, or *exploitation* (I'm not sure which is more accurate). Something happened, though—something quite magical. We connected on all cylinders. We walked, talked, held hands, and ate breakfast and lunch but forgot about dinner altogether until I nearly passed out. One cannot live on love and wine alone! After spending a long, sweet night in each other's company (and arms), we said sad goodbyes the next day, and Leo flew out of Austin to North Carolina—back to the bachelor life he had built since his divorce and retirement from the U.S. Army: church, church, and more church! Clearly, a conundrum was in the making. I had not lived a religiously centered life since I was a child, and I didn't think I wanted to resume living one now. I'd take a long, hard look at this one.

Within two weeks, Leo was back in San Antonio, but I was in Monterey, California, attending my company's winter conference. We had talked countless hours by telephone, but now that he was back in my state, I was gone. He was determined not to let the momentum of our relationship lag, so he sent me a ticket to fly to Raleigh, North Carolina, shortly after I returned home. His aggressive style caught me off guard. I went anyway.

That visit, which was actually to Fayetteville, was very illuminating for me. Leo was not like anyone I'd ever dated. First of all, he was a minister in the African Methodist Episcopal Zion Church. A large part of my visit was consumed by accompanying him while he performed his associate pastoral duties: driving the church bus to pick up and deliver parishioners, visiting sick people, and attending a long Sunday church service. We ate meals in small, local fast food joints and buffet style family restaurants. He was not at all pretentious. This was very sobering.

Though he owned three cars, only one—a well-worn older model Ford Escort—was capable of being driven at the time. This was scary with a capital *S*! Although Leo lived in a sparsely furnished, two-bedroom apartment, we stayed in a well-appointed Marriott Hotel during the two nights I was there.

I knew that Leo had been a career soldier for twenty years. He was retired from the 82nd Paratrooper Division of Fort Bragg, North Carolina, and had elected to stay in North Carolina after retiring and going through a painful divorce. He was in the process of reconstructing his life. He was working as a civilian landscape maintenance man at a middle school campus. Mostly, he was filling in time. He was fifty-two years old and had been married for most of his adult life. His children, like mine, were grown and on their own in life. His heart longed for the stability of a wife and home again. Though he had searched plenty, his search had not yielded anyone he wanted to hold on to. I wasn't sure we could or *should* hold on to each other at that point.

Unlike me, Leo had grown up in an intact family in which his parents had remained married (for better or for worse) for more than forty years. Death and death alone had parted them. They were both gone. When he met me, his hopes were rekindled for the fulfillment of his dreams. There emerged before his eyes that faint possibility of finding someone to love and grow old with as his parents had done. He was going for it.

In February, Leo made another trip to Austin. We had talked almost constantly since my trip to Fayetteville, where he lived. I'd seen his whole picture, and he'd seen most of mine. Neither of us had involved our children in our relationship. That was probably a good thing. Finally, in late February (sixty days later), we decided that we wanted to be together—someplace. I made it clear in a phone conversation that I was not in favor of any living arrangement short of matrimony. I had been single for more than eighteen years, and had not, since Jay, even considered having anyone live with me, nor I with anyone else. I was independent and pretty happy just as I was, but I acknowledged that I still hoped to find the right person to be in a marriage with again. I wanted to take my life to the next level.

You might ask, "Why Leo? What did you see in him?"

The best answer I could give would be: "It was pure intuition." Somehow, I intuitively knew that I could trust him. I had actually seen his face in a dream I'd had just before I woke up early one morning some twenty years before, after Ernie and I separated. It was the face of a very dark-skinned man with a receding hairline. His eyes were small but gentle, and he displayed a broad, friendly smile. It wasn't a face that I'd ever seen before, but it was accompanied by a gentle voice that said: "Trust him." I awoke from the dream almost immediately, feeling somewhat startled. Since I had been frantically trying to find a means of saving my home from foreclosure, I sincerely thought that this face belonged to someone I'd meet who would help me solve that problem, perhaps a loan officer. But that never happened, and I didn't see the face again until Leo showed up in my home all those years later. I had told a few people about the dream over the years, but I'd nearly forgotten about it. As we continued to interact, it came back to me where I'd seen him, and I began to realize why our relationship felt so comfortable. "Trust him," the voice had said, and I did. That was it.

The next day, Leo went out and bought a set of wedding rings for me. I was stunned. When he phoned to ask my ring size, I was speechless. I knew he was serious. We were about to get married. After more talk, we set a wedding date in March to coincide with a business trip I was taking that was sort of en route to North Carolina. It was a practical not a romantic decision.

I winged my way into Raleigh-Durham International Airport on
Saturday, March 3, 2001, at around 5:00 p.m. It was too late to get
a marriage license. We hastily made plans. Leo prepared his pastor
to be on hand for an early Monday morning wedding in the church
sanctuary.

What took place in the interim was nothing short of miraculous!
We romanced each other in a suite in the newly opened motel on the
Fort Bragg army base amid hand-strewn rose petals, glasses of sweet
wine, boom-boxed music, and Burger King hamburgers. We would
get the license first thing Monday morning.

We did take time out to attend Sunday worship service and
to invite parishioners to the ceremony, but the next day, Monday,
we were at the church all alone with the exception of Leo's pastor,
Reverend Franklin Rush, and two of his good friends who had agreed
to stand with us as best man and matron of honor. They doubled as
photographer and boom box music providers.

The ceremony was brief but intimate. We sat on a pew off to the
side of the pulpit and recited our personal commitment to each other
and to our marriage. The music of Etta James' signature vocal, "At
Last," played softly in the background as we looked each other in the
eye, held hands gently, and spoke our personal and original words
that promised love, fidelity, and commitment one to the other. These
were the only vows we would take. When we finished, Pastor Rush
had only to finish the ceremony with the civil part required by the
law. We were husband and wife.

What happened after the passionate, wedded kiss at the altar was
just short of surreal. I ran to the back choir room, hastily changed out
of my elegant off-white pantsuit and strappy satin heels into traveling clothes and a big coat for my journey back to Texas. I grabbed
the beautiful bridal bouquet of pink and white miniature roses and
its matching corsage that Leo had bought for me to carry. I left the
matching, floral-covered comb in my hair. We ran to his little Ford
Escort and set out for Raleigh-Durham International Airport, which
was fifty-two miles away. We had less than forty-five minutes to get
me onto the airplane that I just had to board to get back home. I
needed to get back to Austin, pack up workshop materials, and get
on the road to Brownsville on the Mexican border for a 9:00 a.m.

meeting the next day. This was no small feat. I would drive five hours to my destination once I left my house. After that weekend with my new husband, I needed at least four hours of sleep! Rest, however, was not in the picture. I had to get there, and I had to be ready to present my assessment program. I could have been fired if I had not taken care of this obligation. That outcome would not have been a good one—not for newly weds.

We barely made the flight. The plane was fully loaded, except for me. The pilot, who had been alerted of my plight by the counter clerk's phone call to the cockpit, waited an extra five to seven minutes while I checked in and scrambled up the escalator to the gate. The waiting travelers in our area applauded as Leo and I quickly hugged each other tightly and said goodbye. My bouquet was still in my hand; his white boutonnière was dangling precariously from his lapel. It was another special moment to be remembered. When we released, I ran for the door. We were married, but the bride was escaping.

My kids were frantic! They went bananas.

Ellen called Leo and threatened him with reprisals if he did anything to harm me. In essence, she said, "She has four big kids, and we'll getcha!"

After a while, and after getting a little more exposure to Leo, the kids have all settled down now, and I can safely say they like having him in the family.

Leo and I have now been married for the better part of seven years. He moved back to Austin, and we live together in the house I bought a few years ago. We've weathered a couple of marital storms, mostly over disagreements related to the remodeling of our home (what married couple can't relate to that?), but with the work now finished, we can look back with satisfaction on the results. We enjoy hosting gatherings for friends and family, going to movies and social events, dancing, listening to all types of music, eating out, and watching sports together—as well as participating in some church activities (though he still does more of this than I do). From here, insofar as marriage is concerned, the horizon looks very bright. In our kitchen window, we display a small stone plaque that Leo purchased. On it, the following words by Mark K. Moulton are inscribed

And though they are different in station and form,

their lives are just perfect, though far from the norm.

So if you're wishing for true love, *what's important, it seems…*

Is to accept all the differences…

and to share the same dreams.

-Reflections-

Mention of my beloved wooden porch makes me feel very sad. I built the porch for my mother to give her a more comfortable place to sit outside without being bothered by pesky flies and mosquitoes whenever she visited me. She loved to sit out on the patio and just take in nature's beauty: red cardinals, squirrels scampering through the trees, and beautiful flowers hanging from baskets. She would stay out there all day if I didn't insist that she come inside.

Mama has gone on to heaven. I miss her dreadfully. She never got to meet Leo. On April 13, 2001, just one and a half months after our marriage, she passed away without seeing either "her" porch or her new son-in-law. She had plans to fly here on April 28—there was a ticket in her purse for the flight. But God had other plans for her.

Inspired, I believe by an intuition she didn't share, just a week before her death, Mama requested that I set up a three-way call between Leo, she, and me. Once we were all connected and the salutations were finished, Mama asked Leo if he would pray with her. He complied with the request willingly. He asked her if she believed in God, to which she answered, "yes." He then began to pray a prayer that was reminiscent of the kind I've often heard when people join the Baptist church. She repeated his words that asked for forgiveness of sins and that professed a belief in Christ as her personal savior.

As I listened, I was struck by what sounded like true contrition in

Mama's voice. It was almost childlike. She seemed to be asking him to lead her to some spiritual place that she could not go to alone. When she had said "amen," she thanked Leo and said goodbye to the two of us. I now believe that she had received some premonition of her impending death. It was as if she wanted to make sure that she would be accepted into God's kingdom when the time came.

I wish that Mama could see me now. I think she would be really pleased. I no longer worry about money. I have good investments; a comfortable home; good health; and the love of a warm, caring husband. From here, I approach my sun-setting years with great, positive anticipation. What seemed doomed bloomed into happiness. I awaken each day asking, "What's next?"

Where Destiny Leads Me

Looking back over the pages of my life, I can clearly see how patient, caring, and loving individuals have been integral to my getting to where I've landed in life. It was not easy then, and it is not easy now to navigate through the snares of growing up and to evolve into a life of productivity and charity—especially if you are born black and poor as I was, but it is not impossible. The key, I believe, is that one must have *vision*. I had to be able to see myself in a place beyond the immediate circumstances of life. Vision is the main ingredient of hope. It was the influence of the Hendersons, Dabners, Maxwells, Kivels, Lancasters, and countless others that provided just such a vision for me along the way. Without it, I might never have escaped the low expectations of a Jim Crow society I might have fallen far short of my potential.

Discouragement and depression lurked very near me always, eager to latch on and pull me down. At times, I felt like succumbing to the pressure of defeatism. But failure was not to be my destiny. My dream to stand out from the crowd, to strive for the *extra* ordinary life was seeded in the crowded classrooms of a school called Dunbar. It was a place where people thought I had something special within me and sought to bring it out.

I have since learned that the best of teachers are merely good *coaches*. In the end, the desire to win and the effort to achieve victory comes from within. There are hundreds if not thousands of African Americans like me who have been through similar experiences. They were educated in segregated Dunbar, Carver, Washington, Bethune, Wheatley, Dubois, Banneker, and other schools named for distinguished black leaders of an era gone by. They, too, were confronted with societal obstacles that they overcame. I am so keenly aware that many of them, *so* many of them, are some of the world's highest achievers: scientists, doctors, lawyers, ambassadors, teachers, and artists of every variety.

I humbly admit that I am nowhere near the league of dozens of my black counterparts, and I am very proud just to get to know who they are as that information surfaces. What I have done with my life pales in their light. It is awesome just to consider the greatness of so many graduates of schools like mine. But each of us stands in our own shoes, whatever the size. I have faced many challenges in the years since I attended Dunbar School; some threatened to consume me and others became stepping-stones to a better existence.

Undoubtedly, the travails of marriage and parenting taught me the greatest lessons and yielded the greatest rewards. Some people describe their accomplishments in life as taking place "in spite of" their family obligations, but not I. I am of the opinion that I might not have accomplished nearly as much had it not been for my children. I owe them the credit for motivating me to get up every day and purposefully perform work, to watch out for my health, and to read the good books I've needed to help me understand what I should do to be a good, productive person and a solid parent. It is *because* of them, not *in spite* of them, that my life has been richly textured with substances that nurtured my humanity. From them, I have learned humility. I have learned to hope, and I have learned to fear.

Little did I know when I gave birth, that when I drew those wee souls to my chest, they would not only nurse for my milk, they would invade my heart so deeply that they could literally take control of it for all of time. My personal fulfillment and the fulfillment of my fondest dreams are realized not only through my own achievements but through those of my children that I am privileged to witness.

Of all the challenges, this one, this parenting one, is the most gripping, the most enduring. In fact, I'm convinced it is a virus that, once inside, never leaves your body. Through the experience of motherhood, I have come to understand the deep yearnings of mankind for freedom and for peace. No other mother's struggle escapes my concern, no matter where on the globe she might reside. I care deeply about children, their parents, their homes, and their schools. I want all children adequately fed and properly housed. These are fundamentals that I have scrambled to secure and provide for my children. I know, firsthand, how painful the inability to accomplish just these basic things for a family that depends on you can be.

Who among us did not feel the desperation of families caught in and separated by the most recent storms that hit our nation's shores with unprecedented force? Visions of hearts broken by loss and eyes weeping inconsolable tears will haunt me forever.

Once again I asked out loud: "Is this the end of the world? Is this the work of that Jehovah guy?"

This time, I answered my own question. I now know the "guy" as God. And, yes, I know that this is his work too. I've come to know him as an artist—a mighty and powerful artist. When people, whose eyes he has made, refuse to *see*, he paints them a bigger picture.

This time, it wasn't Los Angeles, Detroit, or Chicago. This time it was New Orleans, where water and wind ravaged an entire city, sparing no one. But, again, it was a portrait that vividly highlighted the plight of the otherwise unnoticed poor, undereducated, and "irrelevant" masses. It is my belief that this greatest of all teachers, God, notices when we need remediation—when we have not mastered previously taught lessons—and gives us opportunities to learn them all over again.

Through interfacing with and helping numerous evacuees of the New Orleans floods and hurricanes, I have come face to face with new purpose. Just when I was ready to retire, I'm finding it uncomfortable to be a standby observer. I've been a soldier in the war against ignorance and poverty since I was a child. I can't quit now. There are new arenas out there—new battles to be fought and won, new landmines to be defused.

If the 9/11 tragedy was America's wake-up call, then someone must have pushed the snooze button in the past few years. With hoards of uneducated, undereducated, and impoverished people spreading out across the country and pouring into our cities—mostly blacks and Latinos—we who are better prepared cannot afford to sleep. Unless and until we all squarely face the future that is being created by a burgeoning undereducated underclass, largely comprised of today's African American and Hispanic youth, the shock of living in a failed society will visit every one of us within our lifetime.

Crystal Kuykendall, PhD, a national spokesperson on the subject, speaking at an educational conference in Austin, stated the problem as follows:

> The schools are not serving our black and Hispanic youth well. Standardized test scores reflect the disparities. Data on suspensions, test exemptions, expulsions, retentions, and dropout rates tell the story of how far too many black and Hispanic students are being distanced from mainstream America. The continued under-achievement and isolation of such a large and growing population is nothing short of a national tragedy. Black youth are being buffeted by a series of forces that, if allowed to go unchecked, could create a "lost generation" (National Urban League, 1986, 1989, 1992). Yet, if this generation is lost, much of our hope for economic, social, and technological survival is also lost. The problem of educating these students must be addressed, or the consequences will be shared by each of us. [1]

In the years that lie ahead, I know what I will do. I will work more diligently where I live to make schools better, more relevant institutions than they are today. That's what I do. I am a professional consultant who trains teachers in curriculum design and effective, relevant, instructional delivery. I will admonish administrators who I work with not to accept crippling mediocrity that masquerades as teaching. I will devote my time and fiscal resources toward the goal of making this a better world for mothers, fathers, and children. A whole world is waiting for someone to care and to reach out to lend a hand to struggling families. In what is left of my lifetime, one of those reaching out will be me.

Just as the angels in my life were a blessing to me, I will—I *must*—be a blessing to others. It's the legacy I wish to leave behind for my children and their children. *Love* is the name of that legacy. Love is the other name for that Jehovah guy. God is *love*. That's a fact

---

1   Crystal Kuykendall, *Texas Elementary Principals and Supervisors' Association Conference*: Austin, Texas, 1992.

I learned from reading the good book: 1 John 4:8: "He that loveth not, knoweth not God; for God is love."

There's enough love for all of us when we pass the overflowing cup around.

As I leave the pages of this story, the details of which I feel I have now adequately exhausted (and beyond), I leave this reminder from my past days as a student attending Dunbar School: the words of Marian Anderson, the renowned contralto, that hung on a banner at that beloved school still inspire me to this very day:

Have a star, and try to reach its height.
All things are possible to the courageous.

CPSIA information can be obtained
at www.ICGtesting.com
Printed in the USA
BVHW042034090822
644147BV00001B/27